D1071797

The Ideologies of Violence

The Ideologies of Violence

Kenneth W. Grundy

Case Western Reserve University

Michael A. Weinstein

Purdue University

Charles E. Merrill Publishing Company
A *Bell & Howell Company*
Columbus, Ohio 43216

Published by
Charles E. Merrill Publishing Company
A *Bell & Howell Company*
Columbus, Ohio 43216

Library of Congress Catalog Card Number: 73-91055

ISBN: 0-675-08835-6

1 2 3 4 5 6 7 8—80 79 78 77 76 75 74

Printed in the United States of America

Preface

In recent years, the subject of violence has awakened a lively interest and a deep concern among politicians, academicians, and many members of the general public. Often such interest and concern take the forms either of seeking the reasons why human beings commit acts of violence or of debating whether or not certain acts of violence can be morally justified. Our work takes a third approach. Rather than identifying the causes or conditions of political violence, or of passing moral judgments on acts of violence, our aim is to explore, theoretically and empirically, the ways in which justifications (ideologies) of violence function in the projects of political actors.

In attempting to realize this aim, our method has been to identify and order the major ways in which violence is justified in political conflict and to show how these justifications are shifted and manipulated in concrete situations according to the power positions of the contestants. We do not claim that our approach is a substitute for behavioral science or moral philosophy, only that it is a needed supplement to these forms of inquiry. Knowledge of how ideologies of violence are used to maintain and expand political power, and to affirm or undermine normative order, decreases naiveté about politics and thereby allows human beings to exert greater independence of judgment in their political choices. Thus, we do not claim that all human beings are motivated by the pursuit of power, or that all justifications of violence

v

or non-violence are mere rationalizations of the will to dominate. Rather, we make the more modest claim that the interplay between political culture, political power and justifications of violence provides a fruitful and relatively uncultivated field for political inquiry.

Our approach does not isolate the study of violence from its wider political context. We do not treat acts of violence as aberrations or exotic outbursts, but as phases of struggles to uphold various conceptions of normative order and to gain or maintain power. We hope that our efforts to link the study of political violence to other major categories of political analysis, such as ideology, power and order, have the methodological significance of supplementing existing approaches and the moral significance of enhancing the possibility for rational responses to rhetoric about violence.

Although many people, living and dead, good and evil, aided us in the formulation of our ideas, we would particularly like to single out for thanks Don Bowen of the University of Illinois—Chicago Circle who gave valuable critical comments on an early draft of the manuscript; Abe Frakas who was an indefatigable research assistant, critic and source of ideas; and Roger Ratliff, Susan Ziegler, and Fred Kinne of Charles E. Merrill, who gave important encouragement to the book at different stages of its development. As is normal in these cases we take final responsibility for the ideas expressed in the following discussion.

Contents

Chapter One

Violence and Political Ideology

Ideology and political violence, the two central issues explored in this study, are complex and multi-faceted phenomena. Neither one of the terms has a single definition upon which specialists agree, and frequently the definitions offered are closely related to deeply held value-commitments. Perhaps the major difficulty confronting the reader of the following discussion will be threading his way through the contrasting and conflicting definitions of political violence. However, doing this will give him the opportunity to reach an understanding of how ideologists use these definitions (and the social functions related to them) to justify the exercise of violence, and how political theories also use these definitions and functions to describe systematically the consequences of violence for human political existence.

   We begin this chapter with a brief explanation of our use of the term political violence, and accompany that with a rough typology of violence. This is followed by a discussion of three important functions of violence, which, in turn, is supplemented by a survey of the types of definitions of violence currently in use. After a brief introduction to the ideologies of violence forming our major categories throughout this study, we provide some impressions of how these categories relate to various contemporary theories of the political process that have been developed to describe rather than to justify the use of violence. The reader should not be overwhelmed by the apparent profusion

1

of categories, definitions, and typologies. It is hoped that the results of an engagement with the ideologies and theories of political violence will be the attainment of a wider perspective on the meaning which human beings give to political violence and a more acute appreciation of the ingenuity with which political actors justify their behavior.

Many of the subjects discussed in this introductory chapter and throughout the substantive sections of the book could just as easily have been illustrated by the work of thinkers and activists in diverse historical periods and from a multitude of geographical and social contexts, but we usually chose contemporary examples, most frequently from the United States. However, this should not preclude an effort on the part of the reader to let his imagination and experience call to mind other, perhaps better, illustrative material. This is what we hope will occur, because we seek to demonstrate the universality of these ideas and processes.

Scope of the Study

Our first task is to describe how we distinguish political violence from other forms of human violence. Given the diversity of definitions of violence and the ways in which different types of violence shade into one another (depending upon the context in which violent acts are committed), the distinguishing features of political violence will be general and relatively imprecise. Some order, however, can be brought to the discussion by presenting a typology of violence and locating the present discussion within it. There are several useful typologies of violence, and that suggested by Renatus Hartogs and Eric Artzt provides us with a convenient place to begin.

Hartogs and Artzt first identify organized violence, which is "patterned and deliberate."[1] All organized violence is instrumental in the sense that it is one means of social combat among many, and it functions in a context of group interests and goals. The second type of violence is spontaneous violence, which is "an unplanned explosion set off by the unique chemistry of internal and external conditions."[2] While organized violence is both instrumental and impersonal, spontaneous violence is reactive, compensatory, or gratuitous. As a reaction, it is a way of striking out directly against frustration. As a compensation, it is a way of making up for frustrations suffered in the past. As gratuitous violence, it is a way of displacing aggression from an object which cannot be attacked (because it is too powerful or because it generates ambivalent feelings) to an object which is too weak to resist and which arouses clear feelings. Spontaneous violence may be collective or individual.

The third type of violence identified by Hartogs and Artzt is pathological violence, which is committed by individuals and has a basis in either physical or mental illness. Pathological violence will not be considered in the discussion of violence in political ideologies. The analysis will be centered on interpretations of organized violence and those instances of spontaneous violence which have significance for the defense, disruption, or restoration of normative order. The study is not concerned with physiological or psychological motivations of violent behavior, although it does touch upon psychological interpretations of violence, as postulated by ideologists rather than by interpretive analysts.

A further distinction is necessary to frame the present study. We propose that organized violence may be divided into criminal and political types. Criminal violence, while impersonal or instrumental, is not directed at the defense, disruption or restoration of a normative order, although it may unwittingly contribute to such outcomes. Political violence is directed at the maintenance or change of a normative order. Nieburg observes that political violence "addresses itself to changing the very system of social norms which the police power is designed to protect."[3] We would add that political violence can also concern itself with maintaining the normative system under attack. However, the distinctions between criminal and political violence, and organized and spontaneous violence are not always clear because all acts of violence, whether or not they are deliberate, can be used for some political purpose. A rise in criminal violence can become an excuse for officials to change the normative system. Criminal bands can become social bandits and finally guerilla movements. Yung-Teh-Chow has shown how this process worked in ancient China: "When a bandit group felt strong enough to challenge the central government for control of a region, it would take the designation of *i-chun*, 'righteous troops.' "[4]

Similarly, it is often difficult to make a distinction between organized and spontaneous violence. Officials can interpret a riot as a political conspiracy, while oppositionists can interpret a riot as part of a movement for change. The present study is concerned with organized political violence and those instances of spontaneous and criminal violence which are used for political purposes. Our aim is to describe the diverse functions given to these acts of violence in political ideologies.

Functions of Ideology

Ideology has been a central theme in twentieth century political thought.[5] Richard M. Merelman has noted that the "uses of the term 'ideology' are legion" and that the best policy for the political scientist is to define the term relative to the specific study he is undertaking.[6] In the present study ideology will be used to mean public justifications for political activity. Ideologies of violence will refer to public justifications of violent behavior in the political process. This definition does not cover all of the major uses which the term ideology has in contemporary political thought. It focuses on the functions of ideology in integrating human communities (defending established normative orders), furthering the position of conflict groups in the process of goal attainment (expanding or creating normative orders), and strengthening the resolve of human beings to engage in political acts aimed at the maintenance or change of normative orders. Many other possible functions of ideology are not germane to the present study. For example, public justifications of political activity can aid human beings in organizing their personal moralities, comprehending the social institutions in which they act, relieving their guilt and displacing their frustrations, and replacing religious belief.[7] These functions, while not inconsistent with those referring to the maintenance and change of normative orders, are primarily psychological rather than institutional in their emphasis. To be sure, when examined in aggregate terms they assume greater public rather than private meaning, but their principal focus is nonetheless individual and hence outside the scope of this discussion.

Defense and Integration

The function of ideology in defending established normative orders and integrating human communities has been discussed by many twentieth century political theorists, among them Gaetano Mosca, Vilfredo Pareto, and Roberto Michels.[8] Representative of this group, Gaetano Mosca used the term political formula as a synonym for ideology. He observed that justifications usually accompany the exercise of power: "in fairly populous societies that have attained a certain level of civilization, ruling classes do not justify their power exclusively by *de facto* possession of it, but try to find a moral and legal basis for it, representing it as the logical and necessary consequence of doctrines and beliefs that are generally recognized and accepted."[9] The political formula of a ruling class is the legal and moral basis, or principle, which the leaders use to justify their various uses of power, including violence.

Mosca observed that political formulas vary according to types and levels of civilization. In primarily agricultural civilizations political formulas tend to be based on supernatural beliefs, while in urban industrial civilizations they are often based on principles that appear to be rational, even though these principles do not correspond to scientific truths. Mosca's most important point is that while political formulas are not scientifically valid, they are not "mere quackeries aptly invented to trick the masses into obedience."[10]

Political formulas "answer a real need in man's social nature; and this need, so universally felt, of governing and knowing that one is governed not on the basis of mere material or intellectual force, but on the basis of moral principle, has beyond any doubt a practical and real importance."[11]

Thus, Mosca defines the political formula pragmatically, by its functions in social existence. The political formula is not arbitrary, but must be "based upon the special beliefs and the strongest sentiments of the social group in which it is current, or at least upon the beliefs and sentiments of the particular portion of that group which holds political preeminence."[12] The political formula summarizes "community of history," and makes the members of a group conscious that they form a distinctive social type. The political formula is an ideology which functions in social existence to integrate the group and to *legitimize* its normative order.

Expansion and Creation

Ideology also functions as a weapon used by conflict groups to expand and create normative orders, and generally to attain more advantageous power positions. Arthur F. Bentley is a good representative of the many thinkers who have analyzed this function of ideology.[13] While Mosca was primarily concerned with pointing out how ideologies function to integrate group life, Bentley was interested in understanding how they function in intergroup conflict. In *Relativity in Man and Society* Bentley summarized his interpretation of ideology: "Everywhere around us parts of our social activity are casting their demands absolutely against the social sky, ignoring their relativity, stating themselves in language-thought structures which split themselves off from their origin in activity and attempt to justify that from which they arise."[14] For Bentley, the staple of ideological thinking is the use of "is" and "must." " 'Is' and 'must' with sneer and jeer and arrogant assertion are the backbone of propaganda, and they hide the weighted value of what is behind the propaganda."[15]

For Bentley, ideology is propaganda, a tool used by groups in pressing their claims for the maintenance and/or extension of human activities. Ideologies are alienative in two ways. First, they deceive outsiders about the intentions of the group. This may be, of course, one of their intended purposes. Second, they may deceive the very people who express them, as in the case of the salesman who comes to believe that his company's product is really the best. In *The Process of Government* Bentley noted a continuity between violence and propaganda as means to the attainment of values: "Muscle is one form of technique for the groups, deception is another, corruption is another; tools of war fortify muscles, and tools for trickery also are to be found." The basis of propaganda is justifying a particular claim for the maintenance and/or extension of human activity in terms of such ideas as national survival or the public interest. In this way propaganda casts group demands absolutely against the social sky and splits language off from its origins in activity.

There is no necessary contradiction between the integrative and combative functions of ideology. While Mosca stressed the role of ideology in integrating the group, he also pointed out that the political formula justifies the power of the ruling class and is not scientifically defensible. Similarly, while Bentley stressed the role of ideology in prosecuting group conflict, he also recognized that successful attempts at deception sometimes led to social peace.

Strengthening Determination

A third function of ideology in social existence is to serve as a means to strengthen the resolve of human beings to act to defend or to change a normative order. This interpretation of ideology has been historically associated with the writings of George Sorel.[17] Mosca used "political formula" to refer to an ideology that functioned to integrate groups. Bentley's term for an ideology that functioned to advance the position of an interest group was propaganda. Sorel used "myth" to mean an ideology that expressed the determination of a group or social class to act: "men who are participating in a great social movement always picture their coming action as a battle in which their cause is certain to triumph. These constructions, knowledge of which is so important for historians, I propose to call myths."[18] For Sorel, the major function of ideology was neither to cement cooperation within the group nor to aid the group in pressing its claims, but to strengthen the wills of group members as they participated in struggles with other groups.

Sorel based his notion of myth on the idea that human beings are self-transcending: "To say that we are acting implies that we are creating an imaginary world placed ahead of the present world and composed of movements which depend entirely on us."[19] The idea of self-transcendence is also the ground of Mosca's and Bentley's discussions. Sorel continued that while the artificial worlds projected by human beings generally disappear from the world without leaving a trace, "when the masses are deeply moved it then becomes possible to trace the outlines of the kind of representation which constitutes a social myth."[20] Thus, myths are not descriptions of things, but "expressions of a determination to act."[21]

Sorel compared myths to utopias. The utopian theorist attempts to construct a model to which he can compare existing political reality. This model can become a design for legislation and can be analyzed critically with respect to its practicability and consistency. While the utopia is made up of a set of imaginary institutions, the myth is a unitary vision of a decisive future event. For Sorel, the most powerful myth of the modern age was the myth of the proletarian general strike undertaken to smash capitalism. He expected this myth to strengthen the resolve of workers in their day-to-day combat with the ruling class.

The functions of ideology as myth are not necessarily inconsistent with its functions as political formula and as propaganda. The same ideology that integrates cooperative activities within the group can also serve to strengthen the resolve of members in group conflict. National symbols, which stimulate obedience and loyalty, may also function as myths in times of war. Similarly, the same ideology that serves to deceive outsiders can also function to boost the determination of group members. The sales pitch which the salesman comes to believe is an example of this overlap. Thus, ideology may function, among many other things, to stimulate cooperation, gain maintenance and/or extension of activity at the expense of other activities, and strengthen the resolve of group members in their struggles. The same ideology may perform one or more of these functions at the same time or at different times. In the study of the ideologies of violence, or the public justifications of violent behavior in the political process, ideologies will be considered as political formulas, propaganda, and myths, depending upon the context in which they appear. Each function of ideology will be important.

Changing Meanings of Violence

The functions performed by ideologies in social existence must be distinguished from the functions given to violence within political ideologies. Within social existence, ideologies function to integrate activities, advance claims, and strengthen resolve, among many other functions. Within ideologies of violence, certain kinds of violent actions are given social functions and are justified in terms of these functions. For example, violent punishment of criminals is frequently justified by the claim that it functions to deter future criminal activities and ultimately secures predictability in human relations. The present study is concerned with the different functions given to violent behavior in various ideologies. However, before these functions can be described and placed in context it is necessary to discuss the various meanings that have been attached to the term political violence. This is not to say that these meanings are exhaustive or mutually exclusive or consistently applied by various participants and analysts. Rather they are advanced simply to make us aware that the very definition of a term and the way it is used sets the framework for discussion and represents an important ideological breakthrough for its users. The actor who succeeds in defining the context of meaning gains an advantage over his adversaries.

In ordinary speech, the meanings given to violence vary according to the wider political beliefs of human beings. There is no single correct definition of violence. The term tends to be defined differently by political actors and sometimes differently by the same political actors, depending on the purposes they wish to achieve, the context in which the term is used, and their relationship to established political authority. Each group of political actors finds the source of violence in a different common experience in everyday life.

Violation

Those dissatisfied with the social structural *status quo* often tend to define violence in terms of the human experience of *violation*. The argument of the philosopher Newton Garver can serve as an example of this approach, which will be referred to as *expansive,* but we might mention that this same viewpoint can be found well expressed in the works of Johan Galtung, Fredric Wertham, and Bruno Bettelheim.[22]

Garver begins his discussion by noting that violence is often connected with the use of physical force: "Violence often involves physical force, and the association of force with violence is very close: in many contexts the words become synonymous."[23] However, Garver argues that the connection of violence with force is superficial. One does not say that a doctor is being violent when he is attempting to repair a dislocated shoulder. The core meaning of violence is the act of violating a basic right of the human being. For Garver, the two basic human rights are the right to one's body and the right to autonomy. Violation of these rights implies that violence has been done.

From this basis, Garver defines four types of violence. *Personal overt* violence is the "overt physical assault of one person on the body of another."[24] *Overt institutional* violence occurs when people obeying orders within an organization physically assault others. Garver notes that it is difficult to assign responsibility for overt institutional violence because while the individual is not acting on his own initiative, "the group does not have a soul and cannot act except through the agency of individual men."[25] *Quiet personal* violence occurs when a human being deprives another person of autonomy through the manipulation of symbols: "If we fail to recognize that a real psychological violence can be perpetrated on people, a violation of their autonomy, their dignity, their right to determine things for themselves, to be men rather than dogs, then we fail to realize the full dimension of what it is to do violence."[26] Finally, *quiet institutional* violence occurs when some people are systematically denied access to social options open to others: "The institutional form of quiet violence operates when people are deprived of choices in a systematic way by the very manner in which transactions normally take place."[27] Garver notes that denial of options is an attack on autonomy and, therefore, constitutes violence. The definition of violence as violating persuasion is not the most widely accepted usage in the West. It extends or expands the definition of violence to its widest reaches, subsuming a number of acts and conditions deemed immoral and heretofore not regarded as violence. As such we can, for our purposes, refer to it as an expansive and ethical definition.

This expansive and ethical definition tends to find the source of violence in the act of violation because those who apply it often want to explain in sympathetic terms the personal overt violence of the oppressed. One way of excusing and justifying personal overt violence is to classify it along with other actions that are called violent because they have some of the same effects on human beings. The oppressed cannot deprive the oppressors of many choices in a systematic way, but they can often resort to personal overt violence. The expansive definition enables one to interpret this personal overt violence as a reaction to the quiet but no less effective and inhumane institutional violence of the oppressor. At the very least one can claim that personal overt violence is no more immoral than quiet institutional violence. When one wishes to make a stronger case, he may claim that personal overt violence is a morally justifiable reaction to quiet institutional violence. At its most ambitious extension, one can claim that it is morally obligatory to smash quiet institutional violence through personal overt violence. In all cases the key to this argument is the equation of physical attacks on persons with institutional denial of opportunity.

These arguments are often disguised by what Bentley called the use of "is" and "must." From the political scientist's viewpoint, this definition of violence is neither correct nor incorrect. The political scientist will agree that physical attacks and institutional denials of opportunity have some of the same consequences for human beings. However, he will not say that the two kinds of activity "are" the same in all respects and "must" be classified together. Those who use the expansive definition often argue that violence "is" violation and "must" be interpreted that way. They seem to be saying that people *should* use violence to mean violation when they make moral judgments. This is not the same as saying that violence "is" violation despite claims to the contrary.

Physical Harm

Others tend to define violence in terms of acts of physical harm. This interpretation is a leading one in contemporary American political thought, and many writers have developed it. We might regard this as an observational definition of violence because it is rooted in the observable act of applying physical force and does not distinguish between the source, purpose, or effect of such acts. Hence, it falls between the expansive definition of violence, which covers physical force as well as other phenomena, and the narrow construction (to be discussed in the following section), which omits certain acts of physical harm.

In his *Public Opinion and Political Dynamics,* Marbury Ogle, for example, argues that the term force can be used to refer to a number of different types of action: "It may be purely physical—an overt individual act, such as the striking of a blow or aiming of a gun, or the activity of a crowd as in the case of a mob lynching. Wherever it entails the use of material, measurable force, we may refer to 'violence.' "[28] Thus, Ogle does not count psychological denials of autonomy and social denials of access to opportunity as types of violence. He is clear, however, that all acts of personal overt force and overt institutional force count as acts of violence and is careful to declare that he does not want to differentiate acts of force committed by people who are not officials: "A distinction is clearly made between the use of force or coercion on the part of an organized, recognized governmental authority and its use by persons or groups not officially connected with the state. In both cases it would seem clear that the same kind of results, physical or psychological, might be expected—from the use of force or violence."[29]

A similar interpretation is given by H. L. Nieburg in his *Political Violence.* Nieburg states that violence can be "unambiguously defined as the most direct and severe form of physical power .... It is force in action. Its use is a continuation of bargaining begun by other means, whether it is used by the state, by private groups, or by persons."[30] For Nieburg, violence is distinguished from force. Force is a "reserve capability and means of exercising physical power" and "amounts to a *threat* of violence or counterviolence."[31]

Like Ogle, Nieburg does not recognize psychological or social denials of autonomy as acts of violence, and claims that the distinction between legitimate acts of force by officials and illegal acts of violence by others is superficial.

The observational definition of violence as "destructive physical action against another person" is no more correct than the expansive definition of violence as violation.[32] Essentially, the observational definition has narrowed the expansive definition to include only acts of violation involving the use of physical force. This latter definition is frequently used to excuse and sometimes to justify certain acts of violence by people who are not officials and to judge as immoral certain acts of violence committed by officials. Thus, those sympathetic with the revolutionary tradition will excuse acts of violence by rebels against totalitarian regimes in which official policies are overtly backed by violence. Counter-violence against tyranny is condoned because the ruling class has not allowed others to engage in peaceful forms of bargaining. At the same time, acts of violence committed by totalitarian regimes are interpreted in the observational definition as illegitimate violations of access to the bargaining process and as violations of the right to one's body.

The ground shifts, however, when violence appears in a regime that pays lip-service to and displays the trapping of representative democracy and yet is bedevilled by pockets of discontent or violent dissatisfaction. The ambiguities of this position become manifest in this context. Here, where social control operates primarily through psychological attacks on autonomy and institutional denials of opportunity, those who employ an observational perspective on violence can see violence committed by disadvantaged groups as either a symbolic demand for a greater share of social values or as an illegitimate attack on institutions for settling disputes which are open to all citizens. Similarly, they may view violence committed by the authorities as either overreaction to legitimate demands or as the efficient use of force to minimize the total amount of violence committed in the long run. The revolutionary stance towards totalitarian regimes and the reformist position towards democratic regimes is, in part, made possible by the observational definition of violence as force or physical harm.

Like the expansive definition, the observational definition may lead to a confusion of "ought" and "is." The key to the discussion of violence is equating force exercised by the state and force exercised by people who are not agents of the state. Like Garver, Ogle justifies this equation on the grounds that "the same kind of results, physical or psychological, might be expected from the use of force or violence." From the political scientist's perspective, there is no doubt that force exerted by officials and force exerted by others have many consequences in common. However, this does not mean that these two types of exercise of force are the same in all respects, or even in all relevant respects. Attempts to prove that the definition of violence "is" or "must be" destructive physical action against another person fail because both definitions meaningfully lead to different interpretations of the term violence. Those using the observational definition imply that their meaning *should* be the standard definition of violence, but they cannot demonstrate that it is the correct meaning, or even, indeed, that there is one "correct" meaning.

Illegitimate Force

The observational definition narrows the expansive definition of violence to include only acts of violation in which physical force is applied. A third usage narrows the definition of violence even further to include only acts of violation in which physical force is applied and which are illegal. This we call the orthodox or *narrow* definition. Sidney Hook has argued in favor of defining violence this way. He states that violence is "the illegal employment of methods of physical coercion for personal or group ends."[33] From this perspective, physical coercion employed by "duly constituted authorities" is legitimate and should be called "force," while the term violence should be applied only to acts of illegal physical coercion.

Allied with this interpretation is the idea that violence is an aberration—an unexpected interruption in the normal course of events. Sheldon Wolin has advanced this point of view. He states that "violence denotes an intensification of what we 'normally' expect a particular power to be."[34] He continues that we designate "acts as violent because the amount or degree of force does not seem commensurate with the circumstances or with what we have come to accept as the characteristic style."[35] Wolin concludes that "violence implies that an unusual amount of destruction will accompany a designated act."[36] A similar position is taken by E.V. Walter. Walter remarks that violence is "generally understood as immeasurable or exaggerated harm to individuals, either not socially prescribed at all or else beyond the limits established for its use."[37] He states that when violence is "socially prescribed and defined as a *legitimate* means of control or punishment, according to the practices familiar to us, the destructive harm is measured and the limits made clear."[38] The basis of the narrow approach to defining violence is, thus, neither the experience of violation nor the experience of harmful force, but the experience of having one's expectations in interpersonal relations disrupted by acts of force.

The narrow definition is based on the grounds that the official use of force functions to support a system of stable expectations, while the use of violence by those who are not agents of the state functions to disrupt such expectations. Underlying this position is the assertion that the use of force is inevitable in human affairs. Joseph Mayer has presented the narrow interpretation with clarity. Mayer, a sociologist, states: "Organization, off hand, is of many forms—cultural, scientific, religious. But underneath them all there is just one type, namely, the organization of force. This is basic. It is the tap root from which all other forms of organization spring and upon which they rest for their ultimate sanction."[39] The socialization of force allows the function of protection to take precedence over the function of defense in human affairs. Adopting a Hobbesian position, Mayer argues: "Protection is the string upon which the social beads are threaded. Take away community protection, and nothing but personal fighting and general anarchy can result."[40] Thus, Mayer traces some important implications of the narrow definition. The narrow constructionists distinguish legitimate from illegitimate force because they observe consequences of force different from those noted by those who employ either the expansive or observational usage of violence. The first group notes that one consequence of force is violation of human rights to body and autonomy, while the latter group notes that a consequence of illegitimate force is violation of the right to stable expectations of orderly interpersonal relations.

This definition of violence is no more correct than either of the preceding two definitions. The definition of violence as illegal use of force and the idea, advanced by Sidney Hook, that power "which has legal sanction and which expresses itself in the imposition of physical constraint as well as in the use of less conspicuous but more effective social pressures, such as discriminatory economic, cultural, and administrative measures, should not be considered violence;" are important supports for a basically conservative interpretation of political morality.[41] They allow the defender of established institutions to claim that the use of force by officials of the state is justified, while the use of force by others is illegitimate, and hence not justifiable. However, this moral argument cannot be made valid simply by narrowing the definition of the term violence.

The three usages regard violence in different ways according to varying consequences of its exercise in social existence. The consequences identified by the proponents of each position help support the general ideological stance. They seem to take it for granted that their definitions are the correct ones. They do not face up to the quite difficult problem of defending the stress that they place on some of the consequences of force rather than others. Are some consequences of force more relevant than others? If certain consequences of force should be stressed more than others, why is this the case? The preceding discussion has attempted to show that the most popular current definitions of violence vary according to ideological position. The present study will not hold any definition of violence as more correct than the others. It will view each ideology of violence in its own context and adopt the definition of violence present in that context.

Patterns of Justifying and Describing Violence

Having shown how the very definition of the term violence changes according to the ideological context in which this word is used, it is now possible to introduce the major theme of this study—the typical ways in which political violence is and has been justified. The central focus for ideologists justifying or condemning acts of political violence has been a political-legal (normative) order which they desire to help create, defend or destroy. When they identify a consequence of violence in social existence ideologists attempt to show that this consequence either justifies or does not justify the use of violence by certain groups. For purposes of organization of materials for discussion, it is possible to see four major ideological justifications of violence.

Legitimist

Legitimist ideologies justify political violence when it is aimed at protecting or restoring a single normative order which the ideologist deems legitimate, or at disrupting an order which he deems illegitimate. For example, many people claim that the state is justified in using protective violence to quell disruptive violence, and others claim that the violence of revolutionary groups is justified when it aims at restoring a traditional normative order. Legitimist ideologies are related to narrow definitions of violence, because they are apt to define violence as an attack on the normative order which they are defending. However, this relation is not logically necessary and legitimist ideologists will often use any definition of violence which helps them further their aims.

Expansionist

A second major justification of political violence is *expansionist*. In expansionist ideologies political violence is justified as a means of imposing a normative order deemed superior on alien groups. For example, an ideologist defending racial inequality may defend the imposition of a political order by force on a racial group he deems inferior. It is important to note here that the term expansionist has an ideological, not a spatial, meaning. The imposition of the supposedly superior normative order may be carried out by a dominant power group occupying the same territory as the subordinate group.

Pluralist

Dialectically opposed to expansionist ideologies are *pluralist* ideologies of political violence. In pluralist ideologies political violence is justified as a means of winning the right of a group to have its own normative order. For example, an ideologist defending the rights of an ethnic group to political and national self-determination may defend rebellion against established authorities as a means to attain these rights. The aim of the ideologist here is not to show why one group should dominate another, but why a group should escape from domination. This ideology of violence is called pluralist because it usually explicitly or implicitly recognizes the rights of all national or ethnic groups to self-determination. This use of the term pluralist should be distinguished from other popular meanings such as philosophical pluralism (the rejection of a single principle for explaining the universe), pluralist democracy (the competition of diverse interest groups within the institutions of representative government), and social pluralism (the presence of two or more relatively autonomous ethnic or national groups within a single society). Both expansionist and pluralist ideologies of violence are related to operational and behavioral definitions of violence because they defend acts of violence beyond those merely involved with protecting a given normative order. However, this relation is not logically necessary and pluralists, especially, frequently use broad and ethical definitions of violence.

Intrinsic

The fourth major justification of political violence is *intrinsic*. In intrinsic ideologies political violence is justified by its direct contributions to the development of personal character, commitment to cause, and quality of social structure. For example, a revolutionary ideologist may argue that if oppressed individuals undertake violent acts against the ruling classes, they will be purged of their feelings of inferiority and become new persons, opposed to the dominant social structure and firmly committed to the society of the future. Similarly, other ideologists of social change may argue that if oppressed individuals undertake non-violent resistance, important and direct psychological benefits will ensue. The term intrinsic is used to describe such ideologies because they tend to justify violent acts in terms of the experiences which they evoke rather than in terms of ulterior aims. Intrinsic ideologies of political violence are related to expansive and ethical definitions of violence because they focus on attaining personal liberation from all forms of oppression. As was the case with the other ideologies, however, this relation is not logically necessary, and intrinsic ideologies will employ various definitions of violence depending upon the particular context.

Violence and the Political Process

The various major justifications of violence can be better understood when placed in the context of contemporary theories of the political process. Theorists and ideologists, of course, differ in the purpose of their thought. Ideologists are concerned with defining violence in such a way that it supports a favored political position, and then with justifying certain consequences of political violence. Theorists attempt to understand the conditions and consequences of violent behavior in social existence and define violence in different ways for methodological rather than ideological reasons.

Ideologists and theorists, then, are both concerned with the consequences or functions of political violence. However, the theorist attempts to *describe* certain consequences and functions while the ideologist attempts to defend or *justify* them. For example, a legitimist ideologist might argue that because one consequence of illegal violence is the disruption of expectations, illegal violence is not justified. On the other hand, a theorist might show how disruption of expectations brought about by the illegal use of violence could lead to the formation of private armies, revolutionary movements, hoarding of goods, and improvement in the political position of formerly disadvantaged groups. Thus, while ideologists and theorists are both concerned with the consequences and functions of violence, their work can be analytically distinguished according to purpose. Theories of violence are important to the understanding of ideologies because they provide the background of political processes and structures which ideologies frequently ignore. Starting with the same definitions of violence as the ideologists, theorists will trace the implications of these definitions through the political process rather than using them as rhetorical weapons. We should not, however, overlook the possibility that ideologists might draw upon the findings of theorists to legitimize their use of violence, or to strengthen their arguments.[42]

Violence in Systems Theory

Parallel to legitimist ideologies of violence are the interpretations of violence which appear in contemporary systems theory. This does not mean that systems theorists are ideologists defending particular regimes, but that they tend to focus on the same functions of violence and use the same definitions of violence as do legitimist ideologists. The standard approach to the interpretation of violence in systems theory is developed in Talcott Parsons' essay "Some Reflections on the Place of Force in the Social Process." Parsons' discussion is based on the functions of legitimate force in supporting systems of stable expectations and of illegitimate force in disrupting such expectations.

Parsons bases his discussion on classifying force as a means of social control. Force is control of human situations "in which 'alter' — the unit that is the object of 'ego's' action—is subjected to *physical* means to prevent him from doing something ego does not wish him to do, to 'punish' him for doing something that from ego's point of view, he should not have done (which may in turn be intended to deter him from doing similar things in the future), or to demonstrate 'symbolically' the capacity of ego to control the situation, even apart from ego's specific expectations that alter may desire to do things that are undesirable from ego's point of view."[43] Thus, force is the use of physical means by a social unit to deter, to punish, or to demonstrate superiority. Parsons states that the central meaning of force is deterrence. It is an essentially negative means of social control, which can compel by actual physical intervention and can coerce by threat of physical intervention. It is much more effective in preventing behavior than in inducing action.

For Parsons, force is only one among many means of controlling behavior. He rejects the idea that any polity resting on self-interest and force alone can maintain stable expectations in the process of social interaction. Human behavior can be controlled through control of the action situation or through control of the motives of actors. Both economic exchange and political power are means of controlling the action situation. Force is merely one type of political power. Further, human behavior can be controlled through the provision of either positive or negative sanctions. Both political power and appeals to conscience are based on negative sanctions. Thus, economic exchange is a mode of control over the action situation in which positive sanctions are provided, political power is a mode of control over the action situation in which negative sanctions are provided, influence is a mode of control over the motives of actors in which positive sanctions are provided, and appeal to conscience is a mode of control over the motives of actors in which negative sanctions are provided.

While force is only one among many means of controlling human behavior it plays a distinctive role in the social process. Parsons notes that each mode of social control can be "foreshortened." For example, Parsons defines power as the ability of a social unit to carry out its plans "regardless of ego's wishes—not necessarily against them, but *independently* of them.[44] Power is "a *generalized medium* for controlling action—one among others—the effectiveness of which is dependent on a variety of factors of which control of force is only one, although a strategic one in *certain* contexts.[45] Force is power foreshortened. Like gold is the base metal for monetary systems, force is the basis of power: "In the context of deterrence, we conceive force to be a residual means that, in a showdown, is more effective than any alternative."[46] However, to carry on the analogy, the effectiveness of monetary systems is not secured by gold. Such effectiveness is founded upon confidence that the economic system will be productive and that money will be accepted in economic exchanges. Similarly, the effectiveness of power systems is not secured by force, but by confidence that those who issue binding directives are competent and motivated to attain collective goals. Power systems depend on the "continuing willingness of their members to entrust their stakes in and interpretations of the collective interest to an impersonal process in which binding decisions are made without the members being in a position to control them."[47]

Force used by a legitimate government representing a "moral community" is a particular means of enforcing directives. When there is widespread disobedience and high incidence of violence there is deflation of the power system. In an economic panic, people attempt to convert their assets to durable goods or gold. When confidence is lost in a power system, there is a tendency to obey only those orders backed up by the imminent use of force. The capacity of the power system to attain collective goals is drastically limited, and officials must use most of their resources to maintain order, or stability of expectations. Parsons observes that the power system of a society is like a bank: "The essential point is that a 'power bank,' like a money bank, is, if it is functioning well, 'insolvent' at any given moment with respect to its formal obligations, in the sense that it cannot fulfill all its legitimate obligations if there is insistence on their fulfillment too rapidly."[48] Thus, the effectiveness of power systems is dependent upon the institutionalization of authority, or the situation in which citizens have made obedience to directives of officials part of their motivational systems.

For Parsons, effective political systems are always making more commitments and demanding more cooperation than they can secure by the use of force. Such effectiveness can be lost in two ways. First, officials themselves can make too many commitments. This kind of overextension is analogous to inflation in the economic system. Second, the directives of officials can be challenged by other members of the society, and there can be insistent demands on officials to make binding decisions "to which the demander has some kind of right but which is out of line with the normal expectations of operation of the system."[49] An example of inflation of power is the case of an official raising the expectations of a minority group and failing to follow through on his promises. An example of deflation is the insistent demand by members of the minority group that the promises be kept whether or not this would involve the use of force against some members of the majority group. A deflationary cycle is set in motion when minority group members take to the streets to emphasize their demands and members of the majority group insist that force be used to protect their property rights. The spiral continues downward as some members of majority and minority groups arm for combat and form private armies. Collapse of the power system occurs when officials can no longer control the exercise of violence by others.

In Parsons' theory the social function of force is to serve as an "ultimate symbolic basis of security," a reserve on which the regime can, from time to time, draw. In the most effective social system negative sanctions are not visible and positive sanctions are present everywhere. This is the case because a stable normative order is defined as a situation in which people have internalized patterns of expectation into their motivational systems. Compliance is the rule rather than the exception, and negative sanctions are only implicitly threatened. People view the force of the state as a means to be used in the last resort, when the other means of social control have failed to elicit obedience. Parsons holds that force is minimized in a constitutional regime because of a tacit agreement among citizens that restraint in demands for immediate fulfillment of promises will be repaid by restraint in coercion of the opposition by those in power. In totalitarian regimes officials are not restrained in coercing the opposition and cannot expect demands to be moderate when there is an opportunity to express them.

In Parsons' thought, force (as distinguished from violence) functions to deter deviations from compliance with the requirements of a normative order. Violence is an attack upon that normative order or system of expectations. Force is one of the many means by which human behavior is controlled and is distinguished from the others by its status as the ultimate symbolic basis of security and the residual means of deterrence that are more effective than any other in a showdown. Parsons' theory of the place of force in the social process shows a theoretical background for justifications of violence in legitimist ideologies, although it is not itself an ideology. That it has ideological ramifications, albeit unintended ones, is undeniable. In legitimist ideologies, the force of the state is justified when it protects and defends an ongoing normative order.

In the works of Lewis Coser there is an alternative functional account of violence rooted in systems theory. While Parsons relates the use of force to the maintenance of a normative order, Coser relates the exercise of violence to the long-run minimization of physical conflict. Coser attacks theorists like Parsons with the argument that "the curiously tender-minded view of the social structure which has generally predominated in American social theory is seriously deficient and needs to be complemented by a more tough-minded approach."[30] He sets himself the task of showing that violence has important social functions. In his essay, "Some Social Functions of Violence," Coser argues that violence sometimes functions as a badge of achievement, a danger signal and a catalyst for social action. In each case violence serves a collective purpose.

Violence frequently functions as a badge of achievement in disadvantaged groups. In highly differentiated social structures in which achievement is rewarded, those who are judged according to ascribed status and are placed at a permanent disadvantage turn to violence as a way of demonstrating achievement: "In the area of violence, then, ascriptive status considerations become irrelevant. Here, the vaunted equal opportunity, which had been experienced as a sham and a lure everywhere else, turns out to be effective."[31] Following this line of reasoning, Coser adds that participation in revolutionary violence frequently offers the actor his first chance to participate in political processes. Further, violence symbolizes the commitment of the individual to the revolutionary cause. By striking out against the state overtly, the revolutionary demonstrates that he is willing to risk his body and autonomy for the cause, and to become a member of a new polity that is in the making.

Viewing violence as a badge of achievement does not take Coser out of the tradition of systems theory. His argument is based on instances of role strain in contemporary society. In the Parsonian view, deviance from normative patterns is likely when expectations are frustrated. The person who is told that there is equal opportunity for advancement and that people are judged according to their merit will experience frustration when he is denied access to values because of his skin color or other ascriptive criterion. One reaction to this frustration is violence. Violence is a great equalizer in the sense that it is the residual of power. Where violence functions as a badge of achievement it is likely that there had been inflation in the power system followed by a deflationary spiral. Using violence as a badge of achievement is functional for a few individuals in disadvantaged groups and for the solidarity of some revolutionary groups, but it is not functional for the maintenance of a society-wide normative pattern. On the contrary, it may be specifically employed in this context to destroy the *status quo*. In the long run it may function to minimize violence if members of the disadvantaged groups are able to gain a stronger foothold in the social structure.

A second function of violence noted by Coser is its appearance as a danger signal, a barometer of societal disaffection. He argues that riots in the United States have "constituted quite effective signaling devices, perhaps desperate cries for help after other appeals had been unavailing."[52] In this case the violence of riots is a sign that more violence will come if measures are not taken to meet some of the demands of the protesting group. Thus, the violence of riots can function to minimize violence in the long run by alerting officials and elites of the need to head off more serious revolutionary activity.

Viewing violence as a danger signal is squarely in the tradition of systems theory. In the terms of Parsons, violent activity is evidence that the officials have undertaken either too few or too many commitments. If they are able to rectify their mistakes before the onset of a severe deflationary spiral, the normative structure will be saved and violence will be minimized. Like Parsons, Coser discusses violent activity within a single normative order. For the most part, in the case of violence as a badge of achievement the members of disadvanteged groups accept the norm of achievement present in the wider society. They are members of "sub-cultures of violence" who breach certain norms so that they can fulfill others. In the case of violence as a danger signal the primacy of a single normative order is even more evident. The rioters are crying for help. They want access to the values of the more advantaged groups and would obey the general norms if granted such access. Thus, violence is a temporary negation of the normative order, not a move to institute a new order.

A third function of violence noted by Coser is its effect as a catalyst. As a catalyst, the violence of some calls forth a sense of "solidarity against their behavior."[53] The commission of illegal acts of violence by agents of the state may "lead to the arousal of the community and to a revulsion from societal arrangements that rest upon such enforcement methods."[54] Thus, the violence of both police and criminals, if publicized, can function to minimize violence in the long run by causing negative reactions in the citizenry.

Viewing violence as a catalyst is also within the tradition of systems theory. There is a difficulty in explaining this function because there would be no need for revulsion against the violence if it had not been committed in the first place. To save Coser's argument it is probably best to assume that the function of violence as catalyst is derived from the functions of violence as mark of achievement and danger signal. If this is the case, to say that violence has a catalytic effect is to claim that there has been a response to the danger signal. From the Parsonian viewpoint acts of violence committed by the police threaten the normative order just as much as acts of violence committed by others. If these acts are made public and there is a revulsion against them future violence will be minimized and the normative order will not be seriously impaired.

At the center of Coser's argument is the claim that violence is a danger signal. In his essay "Internal Violence as a Mechanism for Conflict Resolution" Coser remarks: "Internal violence within a social system may be seen as a response to the failure of established authority to accommodate demands of new groups for a hearing. It is a danger signal as well as a means by which such groups make the demands heard."[55] Further, such violence is an indicator of how serious the group is in pressing its claim. Aside from some ill-developed points about how violence serves to strengthen the resolve of group members, Coser rests his case on the point that intelligent reaction to the first appearances of violence can minimize the occurrence of future violence.

While violence may sometimes function as a danger signal, it is not clear that it always does so or that Coser has substantially revised the "tender-minded" view of social structure. Coser remarks that those in power and authority usually react to political violence by branding it a prelude to revolution and attempting to head it off by resorting to counter-violence. He states that it "behooves the social scientist to point out to them that this is a profoundly mistaken view of the matter."[56] If it takes social scientists to see to it that violence performs its social function, that function seems to be more a possibility than actuality. Perhaps Coser means that violence *should* function as a danger signal. Further, it is in the name of a "politics of nonviolent compromise" that Coser makes his suggestions. It is just such nonviolent compromise that Parsons found to be the virtue of a constitutional regime. Yet Coser implies that Parsons is a tender-minded theorist. When subjected to analyis, Coser's theory appears to become another example of the same genre, systems analysis, with its built-in emphasis on systems maintenance.

Violence in Theories of Group Conflict

An alternative approach to systems theory places conflict among groups, rather than the maintenance of normative order, at the center of analysis. H.L. Nieburg holds that it is incorrect to interpret political violence as either a deviation from a widely accepted normative order or as only a danger signal to elites so that they will be able to make concessions. Violence is an indication that there is a collective quest underway to discover new normative patterns: "Social fits and seizures can be viewed as a form of 'search behavior,' a pragmatic trial-and-error method leading toward new political and social norms that better satisfy the strain toward security, predictability, and low-risk methods of conflict resolution which organized groups require and crave."[57] This view of the social function of violence is based on the premise that "society is inherently composed of competitive individuals and groups, all struggling to maintain or advance their advantages by a wide variety of means."[58] Those tactics which, through a process of trial and error, prove successful in advancing the attainment of group goals tend to be repeated. Thus, when violence proves to be a successful means of gaining advantages it will be widely used.

For Nieburg violence is neither a residual base of power nor a last resort after the onset of a long train of abuses. No social order benefits all members equally, and normative structures tend to represent "the values, interests, and behavior of those who dominate the hierarchical structure of bargaining relationships."[59] The appearance of violence in political processes is a function of the fit between the formal and informal polities. The informal polity, which determines the direction of social existence, is "the concrete and objective bargaining situation that links the complex webs of interrelatedness among all individuals and groups, and maintains or modifies behavior and personality."[60] The formal polity is made up of the rules and procedures which have grown up to recognize past bargaining situations or states of the informal polity. When there is not a close fit between the informal and formal polities the government loses legitimacy and there will be a more or less violent search for new norms.

At the heart of Nieburg's theory is the notion of bargaining. Nieburg holds that bargaining is a process of adjusting conflict through threatened or actual escalation and counter-escalation of sanctions. The limit of bargaining is the pure test of physical strength aiming at the annihilation or complete submission of the other. Most political violence stops short of such warfare and represents a phase in the bargaining process: "The threat of escalation as a deterrent, made credible by actual escalation from time to time, constitutes a claim of dominance or a challenge of existing patterns of dominance."[61] Thus, violence is an integral part of the bargaining process.

Nieburg's most important contribution to the theory of violence is his insistence that violence has social functions different from its consequences as a residual base or a warning signal. While the theories of Parsons and Coser parallel legitimist ideology, Nieburg's thought parallels expansionist and pluralist ideologies. Nieburg holds that conflict and violence can be creative as well as destructive: "Conflict, in functional terms, may be viewed as the means of discovering consensus, of creating agreed terms of collaboration."[62] Violence is the "cutting edge" of social integration. It is the ultimate way of measuring where one sovereignty begins and another ends. Thus, the use of violence is profoundly ambivalent. It defines boundaries which sometimes lead to separation and stagnation and sometimes lead to higher levels of integration. Social existence is defined by competing normative orders and the frequently violent struggle among groups for influence is "society's instrument of creative growth, of continous adaptation and choice among various options for internal integration."[63] Thus, in Nieburg's view, violence can be creative as well as disruptive and symptomatic.

Nieburg's interpretation differs from those of Parsons and Coser because it recognizes the importance of competition among normative orders as well as adjustment and conflict within a single normative order. Parsons does not recognize a creative function for violence. He holds that the direction of social development is away from force and towards power. Coser recognizes positive, but not creative, functions for violence. Sometimes violence builds commitment to a normative order and sometimes it is a signal that a normative order is threatened. However, Coser stops short of saying that violence may be instrumental in attaining normative reconstruction.

An interpretation of violence similar to Nieburg's has been presented by Joseph S. Roucek. However, instead of making the bargaining process the core of his analysis, Roucek offers reflections on the proposition that the "relationship of force and justice is, apparently, a problem facing all ages and all cultures."[64] Roucek notes that some theorists have avoided the "dilemma facing them when analyzing the moral approbation of the use of force by distinguishing between the legal and illegal aspects."[65] Roucek does not accept this line of reasoning and points out, like Nieburg, that "society has a series of accommodations which are arranged like the front lines in such a way as to prevent a complete break-through to the home front."[66] Drawing a similar distinction to the one Nieburg makes between formal and informal polities, Roucek argues that the state arises from conflict processes and survives by maintaining processes of accommodation or bargaining. Dominant groups create states of accommodation, often by force, and constitutions result from new "balances of power."

Like Nieburg, Roucek recognizes a social function for violence. He notes that political violence can be committed in the interest of an outside government or a projected form of government, moral system, or society. Thus, a source of violence is conflict between normative orders. For Roucek, violence can help create new forms of political integration: "...violence is a useful social instrument, especially if we acknowledge that law in the modern state is based upon force."[67] However, he warns that violence is least effective when it cannot create moral sanctions for its practices. Brute force accomplishes little permanent change, but violence backed by moral appeals can be quite effective. The conflict approach places the state on the level of all other groups and thereby makes violence a possible means of substantive change.

While systems and conflict approaches parallel legitimist and expansionist or pluralist ideologies, respectively, there are no current political theories paralleling intrinsic ideologies. Perhaps this is because intrinsic ideologies are oriented more to personality than structure and, therefore, can appear in a variety of political situations. The functions of violence identified by intrinsic ideologists—symbolization of one's character and one's resolve, and symbolization of the quality of the social structure (for example, radicals who brought the Vietnam War "home" to American cities)—are relevant regardless of whether one is attacking, defending, expanding, or creating a normative order. These functions are perhaps illuminated best in theories of mass society which depict isolated human beings struggling to attain meaning in a frustrating and impersonal set of institutions.[68] Violence, then, would become a way to add meaning to one's life and to demonstrate that one was effective.

The following discussion will be based upon the distinctions between legitimist, expansionist, pluralist, and intrinsic ideologies. In chapter two of this study legitimist ideologies of violence will be discussed. In chapter three expansionist ideologies of violence, which justify the domination of one group over others by violent means, will be analyzed. In chapter four pluralist ideologies of violence, which justify force to achieve self-determination or the end of violence in human relations, will be described. In chapter five intrinsic ideologies of violence, which treat violence or non-violence as components of life-styles, will be discussed. Chapter six will contain conclusions about the method of studying ideologies which is implicit in this study and the major findings of the study. In the chapters dealing with each main type of ideology there will be an introductory section describing the arguments involved in the justification and a concluding section illustrating the application of these justifications in concrete political processes. The aim of this organization is to make some of the complexities of political life more intelligible by relating political rhetoric to other elements in the public situation.

NOTES

1. Renatus Hartogs and Eric Artzt, "On the Nature of Violence," in *Violence*, ed. Hartogs and Artzt (New York: Dell Publishing Company, 1970), p. 15.

2. Ibid.

3. H.L. Nieburg, "Violence, Law, and the Social Process," *The American Behavioral Scientist* 11 (March-April 1968): 17.

4. Yung-Teh-Chow, *Social Mobility in China* (New York: Atherton Press, 1966), p. 268.

5. An excellent summary of the uses of the category "ideology" in political thought is Willard A. Mullins, "On the Concept of Ideology in Political Science," *American Political Science Review* 66 (June 1972): 498-510. Mullins puts into context the contributions of such thinkers as Karl Marx, Darl Manneheim, George Lichtheim, Harold Lasswell, and many others. See also, Giovanni Sartori, "Politics, Ideology, and Belief Systems," *American Political Science Review* 63 (June 1969): 398-411.

6. Richard M. Merlman, "The Development of Political Ideology: A Framework for the Analysis of Political Socialization," *American Political Science Review* 63 (September 1969): 750-67.

7. For discussions of some of the functions of ideology not covered in this study see: Daniel Bell, *The End of Ideology* (New York: Collier Books, 1961); Daniel Bell, ed., *The Radical Right* (Garden City: Doubleday Anchor Books, 1964); David E. Apter, ed., *Ideology and Discontent* (New York: The Free Press, 1964); Robert E. Lane, *Political Ideology* (New York: The Free Press, 1962).

8. S.E. Finer, ed., *Vilfredo Pareto: Sociological Writings* (New York: Frederick A. Praeger, Inc., 1966); Roberto Michels, *Political Parties* (New York: The Macmillan Company, 1962); Gaetano Mosca, *The Ruling Class* (New York: McGraw-Hill Book Co., 1939).

9. Mosca, *The Ruling Class*, p. 70.

10. Ibid., p. 71.

11. Ibid.

12. Ibid., p. 72.

13. See particularly: Howard R. Smith, *Democracy and the Public Interest* (Athens: University of Georgia Press, 1960); Harold Lasswell, *Politics: Who Gets What, When, How* (Cleveland: The World Publishing Company, 1958); Elijah Jordan, *Business Be Damned* (New York: Henry Schuman, 1952); Arthur F. Bentley, *Relativity in Man and Society* (New York: G.P. Putnam's Sons, 1926). The combat function of ideology has been the one most extensively analyzed in American political theory, particularly by progressives and liberals.

14. Bentley, *Relativity,* pp. 196-97.

15. Ibid., p. 196.

16. Arthur F. Bentley, *The Process of Government* (Cambridge: The Belknap Press of Harvard University, 1967), p. 442. The process of self-deception is what Talcott Parsons has called "cognitive distortion" in *The Social System* (Glencoe: The Free Press. 1951), pp. 356-58. This characteristic of ideologies has also been referred to by Karl Mannheim as "false consciousness," and by Vernon V. Aspaturian as "institutionalized self-delusion." Mannheim states that "false consciousness" or "ideological distortion" occurs when "persons try to cover up their 'real' relations to themselves and to the world, and falsify to themselves the elementary facts of human existence by deifying, romanticizing, or idealizing them, in short, by resorting to the device of escape from themselves and the world, and thereby conjuring up false interpretations of experience . . . . Knowledge is distorted and ideological when it fails to take account of the new realities applying to a situation, and when it attempts to conceal them by thinking of them in categories which are inappropriate." *Ideology and Utopia: An Introduction to the Sociology of Knowledge* (New York: Harcourt, Brace and Co, 1949), pp. 85-86. Professor Aspaturian asserts, with regard to Soviet ideology, that: "A substantial part of Soviet doctrine consists of abstract categories drawn from what are officially decreed 'facts of existence' through a process which can only be described as institutionalized self-delusion." See his article, "The Contemporary Doctrine of the Soviet State and its Philosophical Foundations," *American Political Science Review* 48 (December 1954): 1055.

17. For a discussion of Sorel's thought and its relation to twentieth-century philosophical currents see: E.H. Carr, *Studies in Revolution* (New York: Grosset and Dunlap, 1964).

18. Georges Sorel, *Reflections on Violence* (New York: Peter Smith, 1941), p. 22.

19. Ibid., p. 30.

20. Ibid., p. 31

21. Ibid., p. 32.

22. See: Fredric Wertham, *A Sign for Cain* (New York: The Macmillan Company, 1966) for an extended treatment of this view.

23. Newton Carver, "What Violence Is," *Nation* 206 (24 June 1968): 820.

24. Ibid., p. 819. For a similar, though more inclusive typology of violence, see Johan Galtung, "Violence, Peace, and Peace Research," *Journal of Peace Research* (1969): 167-91.

25. Ibid., p. 820.

26. Ibid.

27. Ibid., p. 822.

28. Marbury Bladen Ogle, Jr., *Public Opinion and Political Dynamics* (Boston: Houghton Mifflin Co., 1950), p. 115.

29. Ibid., pp. 115-16.

30. H.L. Nieburg, *Political Violence* (New York: St. Martin's Press, 1969), pp. 11-12.

31. Ibid., p. 11.

32. Wertham, *A Sign for Cain*, p. 3.

33. Sidney Hook, quoted in Ogle, *Public Opinion*, p. 115.

34. Sheldon Wolin, "Violence and the Western Political Tradition," in *Violence*, ed. Hartogs and Artzt, p. 25.

35. Ibid., p. 26.

36. Ibid.

37. E.V. Walter, "Power and Violence," *American Political Science Review* 68 (June 1964): 354.

38. Ibid.

39. Joseph Mayer, "The Socialization of Force," *Social Forces* 5 (September 1926): 123.

40. Ibid.

41. Sidney Hook quoted in Ogle, *Public Opinion*, p. 115.

42. For example, in rationalizing South African police suppression of student demonstrations, Prime Minister Vorster quoted "an unnamed American authority" as saying that peaceful demonstrations led to nuisance demonstrations, then to scattered violence, explosive terror, personal terror, and finally general terror. *The Guardian*, 15 June 1972, p. 3.

43. Talcott Parsons, "Some Reflections on the Place of Force in the Social Process," in *Internal War*, ed. Harry Eckstein (New York: The Free Press, 1964), p. 34.

44. Ibid., p. 41.

45. Ibid., p. 42.

46. Ibid.

47. Ibid., p. 46.

48. Ibid., p. 60.

49. Ibid., p. 63.

50. Lewis A. Coser, "Some Social Functions of Violence," *The Annals of the American Academy of Political and Social Science* 364 (March 1966): 18.

51. Ibid., p. 10

52. Ibid., p. 15.

53. Ibid.

54. Ibid.

55. Lewis A. Coser, *Continuities in the Study of Social Conflict* (New York: The Free Press, 1968), p. 96.

56. Ibid., p. 110.

57. Nieburg, *Political Violence*, p. 8.

58. Ibid., p. 16.

59. Ibid., p. 52.

60. Ibid., p. 59.

61. Ibid., p. 82.

62. Ibid., p. 113.

63. Ibid., p. 105.

64. Joseph S. Roucek, "The Sociology of Violence," *Journal of Human Relations* 5 (Spring 1957): 11.

65. Ibid., p. 12.

66. Ibid.

67. Joseph S. Roucek, ed., *Social Control* (Princeton: D. Van Nostrand Company, Inc., 1956), p. 343.

68. See particularly for theories of mass society: Karl Jaspers, *Man in the Modern Age* (Garden City; Doubleday Anchor Books, n.d.); and José Ortega y Gasset, *Revolt of the Masses* (New York: New American Library, 1952).

Chapter Two

Legitimist Justifications for Violence

In chapter one it was posited that legitimist ideologies of violence seek to justify political violence when it is aimed at protecting or restoring a particular normative order that the ideologist regards as legitimate. As such, in legitimist ideology violence can be interpreted in two distinct ways. First, violence may be viewed as an attack on the integrity of a normative order or way of life. Second, under the heading of force, violence can be seen as a way in which defenders of the normative order protect it from attack or restore it after it has been breached. The distinctive feature of legitimist ideologies of violence is that in one situation violence is recognized as wrong and in the other it is justifiable. This is a central dilemma of legitimist ideologies and one on which we shall concentrate in this chapter.

Arguments against Violence

Legitimist ideologists look at political violence in two ways. First, they provide reasons why it is wrong to engage in acts of violence which are not officially approved and in accord with the established normative order. Second, they provide reasons why it is right for officials to engage in the use of force. Thus, the traditional ideologist must reconcile an apparent contradiction. While he must condemn acts of violence committed by those who are not offi-

29

cials, he must defend as legitimate and acceptable official acts which closely resemble in their human effects those which he has condemned.

It is usual for legitimists to condemn acts of violence by those who are not officials without presenting elaborate arguments. Violence is condemned as illegal or as a breach of a more general normative order, and the ideologist simply states the principle of legitimacy, implying that it is not open to question. Thus, in this superficial sense, there are as many arguments against violence as there are principles of legitimacy. Following Max Weber, an act of violence can be condemned as illegitimate because it is not in accord with the will of a prophet, it is not consistent with conduct believed to be intrinsically good, or it violates legal procedures.[1] As long as people do not question the principle of legitimacy, or the right of officials to rule, appeals to the principle may be successful. However, the presence of political violence is evidence that commitment to the regime or the rulers is not uniformly or unanimously shared. Thus, in this respect, legitimacy may be empirically divisible although legally it is monolithic. This means that arguments must be brought forward which appear convincing to the dissidents, the general population, or both. Such arguments rely on describing the social dysfunctions of violence and leave out any discussion of its benefits. It would not do to reduce a defense of the status quo to the more candid aphorism, "We rule because we are stronger," for that would have the effect of sanctioning anti-systemic violence.

Blanket Condemnations of Violence

The most frequent argument against the use of violence is pragmatic. The ideologist simply claims that violence "will not work" to attain the goals of those who use it. An example of this argument is the historian Daniel Boorstin's statement that the "notion that any particular evil, such as poverty, the growth of population or whatever, can be solved by the increase of violence is an illusion."[2] Here the ideologist is appealing to the interests of those who are perpetrating the violence and those who might join them. His appeal is undergirded by two techniques. First, he casts his principle as an invariant sociological law, employing the "is" and "must" that Bentley saw as the core of ideology. Little or no evidence is adduced to support the principle, and it is advanced as self-evident. Second, the ideologist defines the goals of violence in a way that may misrepresent the goals of the perpetrators. (Perhaps the violence of 1968 deplored by Boorstin was not aimed at halting the growth of population.) The blanket condemnation of violence as impractical has little standing in contemporary political theory, for writers like Coser, Nieburg, and Roucek have argued that violence sometimes functions to maintain the stability of a normative order.

A variation of the pragmatic argument is the position that violence will bring on counter-violence ruinous to the perpetrator. An example of this argument is George F. Kennan's statement that violence in the service of social change carries with it "a great and real danger of provoking forms of counter-lawlessness even more ugly and menacing than themselves."[3] Here the ideologist warns the perpetrators of violence that they can expect treatment in kind for their actions. In its best developed theoretical form this argument describes a dialectic of violence. The theologian Roy Pearson argues that the reliance on force is always unreliable: "It is unreliable not so much because someone else may possess or produce a superior force in opposition to your own, but because force contains within itself the elements of its own destruction. Force is not murdered; it commits suicide. It kills itself directly in the ancient sense that all power corrupts and absolute power corrupts absolutely, and it kills itself indirectly in the sense that it begets its own assassins."[4] With regard to the "indirect" sense of bringing on counter-violence, Pearson argues that even if violence gains an apparent advantage, the frustrated victim will not only "return to his former ways as soon as he can," but will also "return determined to repay his opponent for the loss and humiliation inflicted upon him."[5] Like the simple pragmatic argument that violence will not work, the dialectic of violence and counter-violence sometimes applies to concrete situations, but certainly is not a universal law. A variation of the dialectical argument, equally unsubstantiated empirically, is the claim that the use of violence will alienate the perpetrator from people who, in other circumstances, might be sympathetic to his cause. Again, this principle applies sometimes, but not always.

The most extreme form of the pragmatic argument is the claim that the use of violence corrupts the very being of the perpetrator. This is what Pearson means by the "direct" sense in which violence destroys itself. He notes that a basic dilemma faces the proponent of force, because with every act of violence his assets justifying the use of force decay. The ultimate dialectic is that the person who uses violence to redress grievances or to further a moral cause will necessarily end by copying his enemy: "Force sometimes destroys an enemy. It always incorporates within itself the substance of its own destruction."[6] The ultimate dialectic is only open to adjudication by the methods of existential phenomenology. At this point it is enough to say that writers like Frantz Fanon offer an alternative dialectic in which the use of violence acts to purge the personality of inferiority.

It is important to note that the pragmatic and dialectical arguments against violence can be used by others than apologists for a regime. Pearson's essay was an argument against American militarism in Southeast Asia. However, the notion of a necessary dialectic of violence which brings evil upon the violent is a potent weapon in the arsenal of legitimist ideology.

A second set of arguments condemning violence is aimed more at mobilizing the general population against the violent than at deterring the violent. This set of arguments, which was given its classic expression in the works of Thomas Hobbes, is based on the premise that any act of violence aimed at

disrupting the normative order is a direct threat to the conduct of peaceful social relations. Norton E. Long has argued that the logic of Hobbes "sees no
middle ground between anarchy and passive subjection, between full-scale
war and servitude." [7] The Hobbesian position is an "all-or-nothing view
that any attack on government, in practice any infringement of its monopoly
on the use of force, must strike at the foundations of society itself."[8] Whether
or not Hobbes held this position in such a simple form, it becomes important
whenever legitimist ideologies find it necessary to give reasons for condemning violence.

The most rudimentary variant of this argument is the idea that violence is
contagious. Senator George Aiken has expressed the idea in its simplest
form: "If any group or any individual is permitted to engage in lawlessness,
then others are bound to say: 'If they can do it, why can't the rest of us do
it?' "[9] Like the argument that violence does not work, the argument that
violence is contagious is based on taking some of the effects of violence out of
context and stating that violence will always have those effects. The fears of
social contagion and of passionate mob rule are often potent antidotes to sympathy with the violent.

Beyond the idea of social conduction is the core of the Hobbesian position.
Here the argument is that violence disrupts the stable role expectations necessary for human goal attainment. This argument, carried on in twentieth
century political theory by Talcott Parsons, is also central in current ideologies. In Parsons' case, however, there is no implication that every act of
violence poses an important threat to the system of expectations.

One form of the Hobbesian argument is the claim that violence breeds fear
and insecurity, leading to even greater violence. Walter Lippmann defends
this position: "the failure to deal promptly, efficiently and justly with modern violence produces that feeling of insecurity and fear in which more violence is bred."[10] A further development of this line of reasoning is provided
by George Kennan who holds that violence undermines confidence in orderly
procedure and standards of political action. President Richard Nixon has
summarized this argument with the claim that violence is the antithesis of
"those decencies, those self-restraints, those patterns of mutual respect for
the rights and the feelings of one another," which constitute the normative
order of a civilized society.[11] That is to say, violence breaches the system of
role expectations that constitutes the social structure.

The Hobbesian position is the most impressive of the blanket condemnations of violence. However, in the light of the functions of violence described by such theorists as Coser, Nieburg, and Roucek, its scientific standing is in question. While it is true by definition that generalized violence is
disruptive of a normative system, it is likely that some outbreaks of violence
are instrumental in preserving a normative order and others are helpful in

instituting a new normative order. Marvin E. Wolfgang has observed that to survive, "a political culture must maintain a dominant thesis of nonviolence."[12] In legitimist ideologies, blanket condemnations of violence operate to maintain such a thesis.

Condemnations of Violence in Democracy

There are particular difficulties in condemning political violence in democratic regimes. This is because the democratic view sees "government as the creation and agent of society, not as its creator and preserver through its monopoly of force."[13] In liberal democracies, the right of officials to enforce all decisions is not taken for granted. If policies do not satisfy the interests of important segments of the population there is often a feeling that these policies should not be put into effect. In the face of the idea that the government is the agent of society, however constituted, there is emphasis placed by the defenders of the regime on the importance of abiding by formal procedures. Condemnations of violence in liberal democracies are sometimes grounded in the priority of form over content, of procedure over policy.

The standard democratic argument against violence by those who are not officials has been compactly stated by President Richard Nixon: "In a system that provides the means for peaceful change, no cause justifies violence in the name of change."[14] According to this line of reasoning, liberal democracy provides the means for peaceful change through allowing the replacement of officials by periodic majority vote and protecting the rights necessary for attempting to persuade people to change their positions and form new majorities. Related to this argument are two others. First, there is the Anglo-American claim that violence is bad sportsmanship because the good sport accepts losses gracefully, realizing that he may win in the future: "Yet we can maintain a free society only if we recognize that in a free society no one can win all the time; no one can have his way all the time; and no one is right all the time."[15] Second, there is the related claim that those who use violence in a democracy imply that their judgment is infallible. Arthur Schlesinger, Jr. argues that the violent assault on libertarian democracy "is in my judgment wrong, because no one is infallible."[16] This means that violence in democracy is an attack on rationality: "Our process, with all its defects, is a process of change—peaceful change—on which all decency and rationality depend."[17] Thus, the argument condemning violence in a democracy is all of one piece, beginning and ending with the idea that democracy provides a method of peaceful change. Violence is not seen as a direct threat to a normative order, but as a threat to a process through which the existing normative order can be changed peacefully. This is the way in which defenders of democratic regimes adjust to the idea that government is the creation and agent of society. The governed are told that the most effective way of making government the agent of society is to protect democratic procedures.

At its heart, this version of the democratic argument is pragmatic. Its persuasiveness is limited when it is addressed to people who are in a permanent minority status or who are systematically deprived of important facilities and products to which they desire access. These people, who have little hope of gaining benefits, may not be moved by appeals to fair play or reason. Much more likely to be affected by the argument are people who derive benefits or hope to derive benefits from the democratic order. These people will be strengthened in their resolve to condemn violence because they will have reason to believe that their benefits have been fairly won. Thus, those who benefit most from a system of expectations that has grown up within a democratic regime protect that normative order by protecting democratic procedures. This version of the democratic argument is merely a variation of the Hobbesian position.

Arguments in Favor of Force

The other aspect of violence in legitimist ideologies is the defense of force exercised by officials in carrying out their legally or customarily defined tasks. Legitimists usually defend acts of force committed by officials without elaborate arguments. Force is justified because it is deemed legitimate and seen as necessary to protect the given normative order or the process of changing the normative order. However, as in cases where violence is condemned by appeal to principles of legitimacy, simple justifications of force are not likely to be enough when political violence is present. Further arguments must be presented which describe the social functions of force. There are two major arguments justifying force exercised in defense of a normative order. Force is defended as a way of neutralizing violence and as a way of maximizing collective benefits.

Hindering Hindrances

William Ernest Hocking has summarized the argument that the force of the state is justified because it neutralizes violent attacks on human freedom: "Force is indeed the negation of rational human relationship, but it is not the state which does the negating. There are always an undefined number in any society who reject reason and betake themselves to force or are ready to do so: they have already severed human relationships. The force of the state exists simply *to neutralize their force,* thus leaving the rest of society in its natural and human relationship."[18]

From Hocking's viewpoint the force exercised by officials is reactive. It is justified because it is employed against people who have violated the rights of their fellow human beings through taking up violence. This argument is likely to be cogent to conservatives and liberals, but not to radicals. The conservative defines violence as the illegal use of physical force and the liberal defines violence as any use of physical force bringing harm upon human beings. The conservative defends the use of force by the state simply because he considers it legitimate. The liberal defends the use of force by the state when it neutralizes or reduces the total magnitude of violence. Thus, the argument that force neutralizes violence is used by legitimists to win the support of liberals. The radical, who defines violence as the violation of human autonomy and perhaps other rights, is unlikely to be impressed by the neutralization argument. He believes that violence has already been done through structural inequality and denials of opportunity, and that the political violence of those he considers oppressed is best classified as counter-violence. Thus, the radical is likely to turn the neutralization argument around the claim that the force of the oppressed is neutralizing the structural violence of the oppressor. The radical argues that Hocking has not shown that force as physical coercion should be singled out as a violation of dignity.

Pursuing the Good

The force of the state has also been justified as necessary to the attainment of the collective good. R.G. Collingwood has argued that "so far as the ruled are not yet capable of ruling and therefore not yet able to rule themselves they must be ruled without their consent by those who are capable of it."[19] This rule is justified because some people like to be ruled, it is good for some people to be ruled, it is good for the rulers, and it is good for the body politic. Collingwood does put some limits on the use of force. There must be an active attempt by the rulers to educate the people for self-government, and "force and fraud are used by a capable ruler only upon those of his subjects most backward in political education."[20]

Collingwood's paternalistic justification of state force is dependent upon the notion of an objective human good which can be speeded to attainment by the judicious use of force. Whether or not such an objective good is philosophically defensible, the paternalisitc justification of state force is a staple of legitimist ideology. It is appealing to conservatives who desire to protect a normative order in which paternalism is approved. It is normally repudiated by liberals and radicals. However, radicals who have gained control of a government often use the paternalistic justification to defend their use of force in creating a new order. This has led to a misguided attack on radicals who are frequently accused of betraying their ideals after the revolution. However, before the revolution radicals frequently declare that physical force is not always the worst denial of human rights. They simply carry this theme over into the phase of governance.

Extensions of the Violence Concept

The techniques of legitimist ideology extend beyond providing condemnations of violence and justifications of state force. Legitimists sometimes expand the notion of violence in a way similar to radicals.

One of the most inventive expansions of the concept of violence is illustrated in the arguments of the theologian Robert E. Fitch. Fitch reviews three meanings of the term violence. The first and "classic definition of violence is that it is injury to persons or to property."[21] The second definition states that violence is the "use of force in excess of, or apart from the end to be achieved."[22] The third and most important type of violence, essential violence, "is anything that obstructs the legitimate functioning of a person; and it can be perpetrated without resort to either the first or the second sort of violence."[23] Normally, granting priority to essential violence goes along with radicalism. However, Fitch gives his argument a conservative twist by stating that since the self is defined as its interests and activities, organizations (or legal persons) have selves which can be violated. This leads Fitch to the conclusion that certain political activities directed at social change which do not use physical force still constitute essential violence because they obstruct "the normal functions" of government.[24] Fitch's argument, which relies on a particular definition of the self, is simply the most sophisticated variant of the many attempts by legitimists to equate attacks on property with physical attacks on human beings and denials of equal access to benefits. It is well to remember, however, that expansion of the violence concept is frequently a double-edged sword.

In legitimist political ideologies violence is attacked as a threat to the maintenance of normative order or of a process for changing normative orders, and force is defended as a means of protecting a normative order or a process for changing orders. Within this broad classification, however, there are endless variations in particular political situations.

In the remainder of this chapter and in the last parts of the succeeding chapters we seek not so much to understand why violence is employed, but rather to see how violence fits into the ideologies of various political actors. Our concern is to comprehend how violence or in some cases the opposition to violence is rationalized in practical political situations. We are aware that such justifications can, by becoming internalized and undergoing some curious form of psychological transmutation, contribute to the causes and motivations for violent behavior. Ideologies can be at once both dependent and independent variables. The explanation of this linkage need not trouble us in this endeavor. We merely seek to present several instructive, but by no means exhaustive, illustrations of the practical uses of violence and their ideological rationalizations.

Manifestations of violence in legitimist ideology are numerous in today's world, and their variety is astounding. For our purposes, three such illustrations will be drawn upon from three ostensibly diverse regions of the world—the Soviet Union, the United States, and Africa.

Marxism-Lenism

An ideology undergoes a fundamental though sometimes subtle transformation after it becomes a ruling ideology—when it is forced to make the transition from what Mannheim called a "utopia" to an "ideology." This duality of function can easily be perceived when we compare classical Marxism-Leninism as a non-ruling ideology with communist Marxism as the revealed truth for a governing regime. As a non-ruling ideology, Marxism-Leninism is a revolutionary doctrine designed to polarize society and to focus all protest against the prevailing order. It seeks to generate activities toward the destruction and replacement of the status quo. To these ends it rationalizes why its proponents should seize power and why the use of violence is acceptable, indeed necessary, in the struggle for power.

In contrast, as a ruling ideology, Marxism-Leninism becomes a belief system that diverts activity toward the defense and maintenance of the existing order. Therefore, it legitimizes the established order and seeks to rationalize the use of violence to carry out the regime's policy objectives. For these reasons, it is not altogether frivolous to refer to Marxism-Leninism in certain circumstances as an ideology that applies "legitimist," in the sense of status quo, interpretations of violence. To be sure, such interpretations are clothed in a Marxist-Leninist mode of analysis, but nevertheless the designation "legitimist" as we have defined it fairly describes the Marxist rationale for regime force.

Fundamentally, the transformation of Marxism-Leninism from a non-ruling to a ruling ideology has not been a difficult one, certainly not as arduous (philosophically and psychologically) as were those of the French or American revolutionaries. Because the dialectic of history is founded, at root, on the material factors of production, the explanation for purposive violent behavior grows out of the existence of competitive class interests that reflect variegated economic factors. As the productive forces change, a new class emerges to challenge the ruling class that hitherto controlled the productive process in society. It is the struggle between such economic classes that propels the engines of historical change—class struggle, in other words, is the inner essence of history. In this regard when Marx calls upon the workers of the world to unite, it is no less than a declaration of war against the capitalist order—any means that furthers the worker's cause, including violence, is permissible. Even though the ethical standard that gauges right actions is, crudely, the extent to which an act assists the revolutionary cause, that gauge is not as operational as some might prefer. Nor is it an open-ended license to use force at every turn. In fact, Lenin once condemned terrorism (specifically political assassination), but the stated reason was not that it was "wrong" according to some transcendental ethic, but rather because it was felt to weaken the revolutionary movement in expediential terms.[25] Still, Stalin phrased it in a most pragmatic way when, in 1934, he said: "Communists do not in the least idealize methods of violence....They would be very pleased to drop violent methods if the ruling class agreed to give way to the working class."[26] The overwhelming thrust of Lenin's and Stalin's guidance was to encourage the use of violence when it furthered the party and the revolution.

But there is, nonetheless, an underlying ethic in the Marxist use of violence. The Hegelian dialectic posits the reality of continual change. Eternal, immutable principles and ideals, like "facts," are subject to constant alteration. Moral standards based upon some putative transcendent order are at best a figment of bourgeois imagination, at worst a conscious effort to divert the masses from their class identity. So, in rejecting a universal abstract ethical ideal, Marx and his followers contended that standards of good and bad are and must be rooted in the economic character of the social organism. The class struggle created an ethic all its own.[27] Standards of morality thus, in any given society, are the standards of the dominant class.[28] In the words of Engels: "And as society has hitherto moved in class antagonisms, morality was always as a class morality...."[29] But a class morality, presumably one created by and for a given class, is something different from the Leninist conception of class morality. In a 1920 address he phrased it this way:

> We deny all morality taken from superhuman or non-class conceptions. We say that this is a deception, a swindle, a befogging of the minds of the workers and peasants in the interests of the landlords and capitalists.
>
> We say that our morality is wholly subordinated to the interests of the class-struggle of the proletariat. We deduce our morality from the facts and needs of the class-struggle of the proletariat.[30]

There is a subtle distinction between a proletarian morality and a morality that functions in the interests of the proletariat. The first implies an immutable morality. The second is bound up with the challenge of perception and interpretation. For interests are not always intelligible, even by those in whose interest a morality is ostensibly derived. The matter of interpretation of interest then becomes all important. If we accept the Leninist argument advanced in *What Is To Be Done?*(1902) in which he rejects the "spontaneity" of the working-class ideas and actions,[31] we thus question the ability of the working class to provide its own leadership. In this way Leninists implicitly underscore the distinction between a class morality and a morality devised in the interests of that class as determined by a particular group who has the right to speak for that class, by virtue of some particular interpretation of history.

It is precisely in this context that the Bolsheviks grappled with issues of violence. In brief, they became obliged to preface each variety of violence with class nomenclature, that is, to speak of bourgeois violence and proletarian violence in order to assign a value to each particular act. In practical application, giving class designations to violent behavior can be controversial, even among Marxists. When, for example, Stalin sought to purge the Party of his enemies, the charges and prosecution were couched in class terms—the accused became enemies of the working-class or those allied with enemies of the working-class. Thus their removal was legitimized. They allegedly schemed to betray the revolution, and thereby became apt targets for regime retribution. Hence, real historical meaning is given to the punishments they suffered, and the justification for the terror of the purges seeks to spin reason out of the thread of unreason. Progressive violence supplants regressive violence. History and violence have purpose, or so they would have it.[32]

But it must be recalled that when Premier Nikita Khrushchev denounced Stalin at the Twentieth Party Congress in 1956, it was not so much Stalin's ruthlessness, dishonesty, arbitrariness, and perfidiousness that Khrushchev criticized, but that Stalin applied these devices to members of his own Party, his class allies. Indeed, Stalin was praised for the victories over capitalism and imperialism during his stewardship of the Soviet Union.

Likewise, the issue of identifying properly the class component of violence is a difficult one, though crucial, in dealings among fraternal communist parties. Again Stalin came under fire for exploiting so-called "selfless economic aid and assistance" to other Socialist countries. He violated class-based norms that he should have understood and respected. The 1968 invasion of Czechoslovakia has also been criticized by non-Soviet communists along similar lines, and it has been defended by Soviet officials in class terms as well. According to General Secretary Leonid Brezhnev, the "danger of right-wing revisionism . . . paves the way for the penetration of bourgeois ideology." Thus in the 1968 Czechoslovakian case, the USSR and the "fraternal Socialist countries then jointly took the decision to render internationalist assistance to Czechoslovakia in defense of socialism. In the extraordinary conditions created by the forces of imperialism and counter-revolution, we were bound to do so by our class duty, loyalty to socialist internationalism and the concern for the interests of our states and the future of socialism and peace in Europe."[33] For socialist read proletarian and for socialism read rule by the proletariat and the class component becomes more evident. Even so there is a clear departure from classical Marxism-Leninism with the appeal to the "interests of our states."

We can see, then, that the discernment of the "correct" line, that the "correct" recognition of class interests, is subject to varying interpretation in practice and that the regime benefits by making distinction between class violence and violence in the interests of that class. For when there is division as to whether or not a given violent act can be justified, it is the Communist Party as the proclaimed vanguard and organized weapon of the working-class, the "highest form of the class association of the proletariat," and the embodiment of its "unity of will," that make the final determination.[34] The Party leads the proletariat in the name of a particular conception of the proletariat which follows from the Marxist philosophy of history. This conception of the proletariat does not always coincide with the expressed and/or unstated will and sentiment of the proletariat at any given moment. And within the Party, it is the top leadership, as chosen according to the principles of democratic centralism, who guide and thereby speak for the proletariat.

Now, in international dealings involving socialist states, the Communist Party of the Soviet Union defines relationships that include coercion and interference by the USSR in terms of intra-party relationships. Thus, when intervention is employed, it is, ideologically and legalistically speaking, merely one organization of the proleteriat dealing with another. Theoretically, the Soviet state is not interfering in the affairs of another socialist state. Although the 1968 Brezhnev Doctrine may have altered this position, and in the long run Soviet theoreticians may regret the new nuances, the basic class component still prevails in most Soviet applications of force in defense of the status quo, domestic as well as external. The institutionalization of an ideology can evolve smoothly into a special brand of pragmatism.

The United States

Legitimist images of violence are far more ambiguous in the context of American politics. They are, on the one hand, widely subscribed to and more explicable given the history of the almost two hundred years of United States governmental continuity and the essentially British cultural and philosophical heritage. The view that the use of violence in disturbing the normative order (the "American way of life") is illegal and immoral, and the use of force in enforcing the laws of society and particularly in suppressing violent dissent (and often other forms of disruptive non-violent dissent and civil disobedience) is almost an article of faith among public officials and a large majority of the American citizenry. Those who face the regime with such intensity of opposition as to risk and even to plan for the use of force to disrupt or overthrow the established order have, *ipso facto,* placed themselves outside the American pale.

Though it may seem trite to repeat them here, there are certain vague but deeply embedded principles in the American political style that enable the leaders and the led of America to banish to a political purgatory those who would use violence to disturb the system. Thus the tendencies to be empirical and pragmatic, to eschew ideologues and be suspicious of wholistic models, to be problem solvers and to regard all problems as solvable, to prefer "reason" (meaning bargaining; "Come, let us reason together"), compromise, and consensus, and to regard agreement on the "rules of the game" as the measure of sportsmanship necessary to keep the social fabric intact are integral parts of politics in this liberal democracy. To be sure, America on occasion has departed radically from these patterns domestically (e.g., the Civil War and the treatment of various minorities in World Wars I and II) and in her foreign policies. But by and large these features comprise the common stock of popular impressions of American politics, and they often impose implicit limitations on just what the government may and may not do to maintain the system. They are, after all, a reflection of a socio-political structure that was regarded to be, in the formative years, relatively homogeneous. Where division existed it was either ignored or through a process of cognitive distortion glossed over by those who were of the majority. One could argue that Barry Goldwater's candidacy for the Presidency in 1964 was something of a shock to the American public because he functioned in a different, more ideological, gear than did any of his predecessors. A case could be made as well that he was rejected because he stepped forward too soon, historically speaking. In many ways, Goldwater presaged a changing temper in America, a temper that found a more "acceptable" though no less harsh representation in the utterances of Spiro Agnew.

Those who advocate the use of violence to change the American way are branded as "un-American" (an unbelievably useful and appropriate appellation because it carries with it a plethora of normative and prudential corollaries), abnormal, aberrant and hence to be neutralized if not removed from the political scene. For example, in the January 6, 1969 Harris Survey entitled "Hopes and Expectations of Protest," 90 percent of the public surveyed favored a crack down on hippie and student protest groups, and 86 percent approved of a crack down on Viet Nam war protesters.[39] As if to echo this, a few months later the U.S. Deputy Attorney General Richard Kleindienst was quoted as saying, "If people demonstrate in a manner to interfere with others, they should be rounded up and put in a detention camp."[35] In periods of domestic and external stress the "law and order" theme, in one form or another, dominates the symphony.

Even so, an ambiguity surfaces. There is a general uneasiness in the employment of legitimate force against proponents of change. Even some who defend the use of the coercive arm of the state do so reluctantly, with a sense that its employment constitutes a testimony that somehow the American system has failed. This uneasiness grows as well out of the ostensible dedication to the constitutional principles of limited government and the widespread, often fuzzy dedication to the virtues of pluralism and distrust of big government. Thus the very principles and style of American politics that ostracize and reject those who use violence to upset the status quo also make for the reticence to employ too blatantly the use of force to suppress dissent that represents a challenge to a stable order. Moreover, there is often a gnawing impression in America, particularly among liberals who defend the regime's use of force in certain cases, that what violent revolutionaries seek or pretend to seek (racial equality, group identity, an influential voice in fundamental decisions that directly affect their lives, a more equitable distribution of America's wealth and resources, and an end to foreign military activities) may be just, equitable, and necessary. They find themselves uncomfortable in the same camp as those who defend regime force because of selfish or anti-humanistic sentiments or because they oppose the specific policy goals of the anti-regime movements. Take, for example, *Time* magazine's position regarding the use of police force against the Black Panthers. *Time* argues that "Society has a duty to defend itself against private armies; there can be no argument that Panther arms caches should be broken up just like those of the Mafia or the Ku Klux Klan or the Minutemen." Nevertheless, in the case of the December, 1969 raid by policemen attached to the State's Attorney's office in Chicago which resulted in the deaths of two Panther leaders, *Time* was clearly critical of police tactics. In this case *Time* argued that "the special history of injustice to blacks" in America demanded a different approach to the situation.[37] At once this was a rationalization for the employment of force and yet an embarrassment that it had to come to forceful repression. Such awkwardness results, then, because many Americans have never made their peace with ideologically unorthodox opposition to the regime.

Regime force, though legitimate, is employed, so the popular reasoning runs, only as a last resort. In the United States the traditional defense of its use depends upon a reactive rationale. The view that "You started it; so we must finish it" almost passes for conventional philosophical wisdom. Once the danger to the system is manifest, in the eyes of the regime and its supporters, force is justifiably applied. Thus J. Edgar Hoover could argue in the defense of police repression of the Black Panthers that of all the "black extremist groups," "the Black Panther Party, without question, represents the greatest threat to the internal security of the country."[38] To the Panther charge that there was a nationwide and coordinated plan to eliminate the Black Panther Party, police spokesmen responded in essentially two ways. They argued, inversely, that the Panthers (often in concert with violent white groups) were plotting a guerrilla war against the system.[39] Or they voiced the less structural and more personal reaction that there was no police plot. Police action "is a perfectly natural reaction by a policeman facing someone who has said, even boasted, that he is prepared to shoot it out."[40] A capsule expression of these explanations can be found in a statement by a Los Angeles police official:

> We are only trying to enforce the law. The Panthers or any other group are welcome to exist as long as they obey the law. But when they stockpile weapons and commit assaults on police and citizens, then it is our duty to act.[41]

In summary, it should be evident that American categories of acceptable violent behavior are far more murky than Soviet Marxist ones which, themselves, are unclear, despite their putative doctrinal clarity.

Africa

Numerous other examples of legitimist modes of thought about violence can be found in the most unlikely places—we are assuming they are obvious in the likely places. In professedly revolutionary African socialist states, for example, regimes that see the need for the selective use of violence in bringing themselves to power, and the massive use of violence in ending colonial and white-dominant systems in Southern Africa, reject its use against their own systems, and sanction the use of regime force to quash public and sometimes private dissent and criticism. The defense of single-party rule, preventive detention, government by executive decree, rigorous censorship and police surveillance of potential as well as real dissidents employs at base an essentially legitimist rationalization for regime coercion. Reference to a "national emergency," and to the dangers of subversion by external powers is common. "In fledgling states," wrote one leader, "imperialist interests flourish where there is an atmosphere of dissension. They are endangered in an atmosphere of national unity and stability."[42] He asked himself: Could his country afford the luxury of all the individual liberties which the established democracies had taken generations to evolve? Apparently the answer was an emphatic negative.[43] His reasoning ran something like this: I am the party; the party is the nation; therefore, anything that weakens or threatens my continued rule is dangerous to the nation. By identifying dissent and criticism of the regime with neo-colonialism, he managed to lend an aura of morality to the coercive and perfectly pragmatic suppression of civil liberties and the concentration of power in his own hands. By identifying dissent with external loyalties and thereby making it treasonous, practically any measure of regime force is justifiable. The same device has been employed by the right-wing in the United States. As Hermann Goering is reported to have said: "Voice or no voice, the people can always be brought to do the bidding of the leaders. All you have to do is tell them they are being attacked and denounce the pacifists or lack of patriotism."[44] Similar perspectives on regime violence can be found in the various manifestations of "guided democracy" as practiced in other developing countries, both professedly revolutionary and openly conservative.

Summary

What can be demonstrated from the foregoing discussion is the central dilemma facing politicians who employ a legitimist interpretation of violence. There would appear to be an inherent contradiction built into any perspective that says, in effect, that violence is both good and bad. It would appear further that they must somehow reconcile this contradiction. The Marxist, employing a Hegelian unity of opposites, gets around this problem neatly, though in its practical application questions abound. The liberal democrat and his relatives have more difficulty. In his mind violence is good if it defends the system he controls. It is bad if it is used against an order from which he benefits. But this argumentation is a little too candid for most to live with. So other devices are utilized. He subtly begins to use two separate words—violence and force. Violence by definition is bad; force is good. Thus, he studiously avoids the use of the word violence in referring to regime actions. Force, characteristically regime behavior, no longer is a synonym for violence. It is not even a species of the genus violence. It becomes something qualitatively different. So far, however, the terminological transformation is not complete. His second line of rationalization is to insist that the use of regime force is purely reactive rather than initiatory. We use force, he pleads, only because they used it first. It is only a short step from this position to be the one that sanctions preventative force: we use force because they were getting ready to strike first. Thus this latter argument is less common. A third line of argument is to couch coercive regime behavior in legalistic rhetoric. We are legally empowered to defend the order. If they want to change the system, let them go through the legitimate channels provided for peaceful change. This, by far, is the most widespread legitimist rationale. There are some legitimists who at heart would like to invoke the *ultima ratio regum* and say simply, we may employ force because we have a monopoly on the legitimate use of force and because we are stronger. This, in the long run, is a dangerous argument. If legitimacy rests, in the final analysis, on the force of arms, the avenue is open for any contending groups to resist the regime by positing their legitimacy on precisely the same grounds—we intend to displace you by becoming stronger; when this is consummated we rightfully deserve to rule.

Legitimists, ambivalent about the use of violence, would be compelled to defend their system with no holds barred. The result could well be an evolution into other, non-legitimist justifications for violent behavior.

NOTES

1. Max Rheinstein, ed., *Max Weber on Law in Economy and Society* (New York: Simon and Schuster, 1967), p. 1.

2. Daniel J. Boorstin, "Violence Can Only Destroy Us," *U.S. News and World Report,* 17 June 1968, p. 34.

3. George F. Kennan, "A 'Liberal' Looks at Violence in U.S. and Where It's Leading," *U.S. News and World Report,* 17 June 1968, p. 66.

4. Roy Pearson, "The Dilemma of Force," *The Saturday Review,* 10 February 1968, p. 24.

5. Ibid., p. 24.

6. Ibid., p. 55.

7. Norton E. Long, "Political Violence," *Journal of Human Relations* 13 (1965): 411-12.

8. Ibid., p. 412.

9. George Aiken, "Law and Order Must be Restored," *U.S. News and World Report,* 17 June 1968, p. 11.

10. Walter Lippmann, "On Order and Justice," *Newsweek,* 11 July 1968, p. 19.

11. Richard M. Nixon. "Responsible University Leadership." *Vital Speeches* 36 (1 October 1970): 739.

12. Marvin E. Wolfgang, "A Preface to Violence," *The Annals of the American Academy of Political and Social Science* 364 (March 1966): 3.

13. Long, "Political Violence," p. 412.

14. Nixon, "Responsible University Leadership," p. 739.

15. Ibid., p. 738.

16. Arthur Schlesinger, Jr., "Violence 1968," *Harper's,* August 1968, p. 23.

17. Ibid., p. 20.

18. William Ernest Hocking, *Man and the State* (Hamden, Conn.: Archon Books, 1968), p. 59.

19. R.G. Collingwood, *The New Leviathan* (Oxford: The Clarendon Press, 1942), p. 203.

20. Ibid., p. 205.

21. Robert E. Fitch, "The Uses of Violence," *The Christian Century* 85 (17 April 1968): 483.

22. Ibid., p. 483.

23. Ibid., p. 483.

24. Ibid., p. 484.

25. V.I. Lenin, *Left-Wing Communism: An Infantile Disorder* (New York: International Publishers Company, 1940).

26. Byron Dexter, "Clausewitz and Soviet Strategy," in *The Soviet Union: 1922-1962,* ed. Philip E. Mosely (New York: Frederick A. Praeger, 1963), p. 287.

27. For a fuller discussion of these points, see R.N. Carew Hunt, *The Theory and Practice of Communism: An Introduction* (Baltimore: Penguin Books, 1963), pp. 109-22.

28. Friedrich Engels, *Herr Eugen Duhring's Revolution in Science: Anti-Duhring* (New York: International Publishers, n.d.), pp. 109-10.

29. Ibid., p. 109.

30. Speech to the Third All-Russian Congress of the Young Communist League of the Soviet Union, reprinted in *The Soviet Crucible: Soviet Government in Theory and Practice,* ed. Samuel Mendel (Princeton, N.J.: D. Van Nostrand Co., 1959), pp. 174-75.

31. What Is To Be Done?: Burning Questions of our Movement (New York: International Publishers, 1943), pp. 31-53, 72-93.

32. Maurice Merleau-Ponty, *Humanism and Terror: An Essay on the Communist Problem,* trans. John O'Neill (Boston: Beacon Press, 1969), esp. 1-98.

33. Excerpts from Brezhnev's Report to the 24th Party Congress of the CPSU reprinted in *New York Times,* 31 March 1971, p. 14. Italics added.

34. See Hunt, *Theory and Practice,* pp. 185-92.

35. As cited in *Dissent in Crisis: The Anti-Riot Act* (New York: American Civil Liberties Union, n.d. [1970?]), p. 3.

36. As quoted by Elizabeth Drew, "Reports: Washington," *Atlantic,* May 1969, p.11.

37. *Time,* 19 December 1969, p. 16.

38. As quoted in "A Close Look at 'Black Panther' Shootouts," *U.S. News and World Report,* 22 December 1969, p. 25.

39. Ibid.

40. As quoted in *Time,* 19 December 1969, p. 15. On the specifics of the charges levelled by Panther counsel Charles R. Garry, see the careful article by Edward Jay Epstein, "The Panthers and the Police: A Pattern of Genocide?" *The New Yorker,* 13 February 1971, pp. 45-77.

41. As quoted in *U.S. News and World Report,* 22 December 1969, p. 26. See also Louis H. Masotti and Jerome R. Corsi, *Shootout in Cleveland: Black Militants and the Police—July 23, 1968* (New York: Bantam Books, 1969) for a revealing treatment of police attitudes to Black nationalist groups.

42. Kwame Nkrumah, *Africa Must Unite* (New York: Praeger, 1963), p. 76. An elaboration of the following points can be found in Kenneth W. Grundy, "The Political Ideology of Kwame Nkrumah," in *African Political Thought: Lumumba, Nkrumah, and Toure,* ed. W.A.E. Skurnik (Denver: University of Denver, 1968), Monograph Series in World Affairs 5 (1967-68): 65-100.

43. Ibid., 72-78.

44. As quoted in Arnold Wolfers, "The Pole of Power and the Pole of Indifference," reprinted in *International Politics and Foreign Policy,* ed. James N. Rosenau (New York: The Free Press, 1969), rev. ed, p. 178.

Chapter Three

Violence in Expansionist Ideologies

Justifications of violence in legitimist ideologies are based on the distinction between force and violence. The legitimist uses the term force when physical harm is done by officials to enemies of the established normative order, and the term violence when attacks are launched against the established normative order. Legitimists rely heavily on the distinction between force and violence because they attempt to justify some acts of physical harm and condemn others. They cannot simply state that the might behind the established order is sufficient justification for official actions. If might made right, the revolutionary would be as justified as the official in using the means to physical harm.

Legitimist justifications of violence are most successful where one normative order is widely accepted and there is a broad consensus defining the officials as legitimate protectors of that order. Under such conditions those who attack the normative order are defined by most people as deviants who deserve whatever punishment the officials choose to mete out. When such a consensus on the order itself and the legitimacy of those who administer it is not present, legitimist justifications of violence are likely to be less effective. Many defenders of tradition will turn to new patterns of thought based on justifying violence as a means to insuring the survival and/or expansion of a reputedly superior normative order. These patterns of thought comprise the *expansionist* mode in the justification of violence.

47

Transition of the Expansionist Mode

The transition from the legitimist mode of thought to the expansionist is sparked by the encounter between competing normative orders. The idea that "East is East and West is West," or that a "proletarian" morality is somehow different from a "bourgeois" morality, leads to the possibility that many people will not take for granted the validity of a traditional and established normative order. The notion that some normative order must be enforced if human beings are to live and prosper may not be enough to convince people that the traditional order is worthy of support. A competing way of life might be more appealing to large and potentially powerful segments of the general population. If there are competing normative orders and no established code is taken to be valid as a matter of course, proponents of each competing order strive to persuade others that their code is superior to the opposing codes. This means that legitimists are drawn into the general struggle. They can no longer stand above violence and defend the judicious use of force. They may give up the distinction between force and violence and defend violence in the service of a superior order.

Francis W. Coker has given an insight into the dynamics of the transition from legitimist to expansionist modes of justifying violence. Coker notes that economic, social, and religious groups whose interests are served by existing law "most readily appreciate the advantages of respect for legal authority; they are foremost in invoking the full force of government to suppress private violence and restrain outspoken criticism of the law."[1] However, he continues, when such interests are threatened "the authority of the interest may be rated higher than that of the law; the advocate of "law and order" becomes contemptuous of law and may advocate disorder or even armed rebellion."[2] Coker concludes that "not every publicist who advises respect for order and authority is opposed to violence or illegality as such."[3] When a traditional interest is threatened and its advocates resort to violence, they do not normally justify their activities simply on the grounds that might makes right. They tend to moralize and rationalize their activities by an appeal to "higher principles." Violence is justified because it is applied in the service of a superior normative order. The process of phasing from the legitimist to the expansionist mode is gradual and often confused, but it occurs nonetheless.

The Roots of the Expansionist Mode

Legitimist ideologies are based on a careful attention to the relation between ends and means. For the legitimist, the end emphatically does not justify the means. Only those means approved within the established normative order can be legitimately used. This is the ground of the legitimist's distinction between force and violence. Certain uses of force are legitimate within the normative order; acts of violence are illegitimate.

Double-Morality

The legitimist who moves outside of the normative order to protect a threatened interest must take the position that the end justifies the means. In adopting this stance, he becomes committed to what William Ernest Hocking called a "double-morality." For Hocking, a double-morality means that members of one's own group are treated according to one standard, while members of other groups (deemed inferior in some way) are treated according to another standard of conduct. Hocking thought that the double-morality was particularly characteristic of the modern age in which the encounter between diverse cultural traditions and the proliferation of specialities cut human beings loose from their moorings in tradition. Without authoritative standards to guide their conduct, human beings turned to one or another of the groups around them. Within the group a strict code of loyalty is enforced: "loyalty implies an intimate sense of *unity of purpose* with the group: a disloyal act, even a deception or silent reserve of the truth, disturbs the integrity of that inner sense."[4] Outside of the group, loyalty to group interest, "whatever it involves to the outer impediment, becomes the *first and inclusive moral law*."[5] The double-morality has a powerful psychological support: "It is not simply one's duty that is involved: one's happiness is involved also, since life with the group becomes part of one's at-home-ness in the world, and of one's self-realization."[6] Through the device of the double-morality the doctrine that the end justifies the means became a respectable part of the expansionist's ideology.

Rework Tradition

Another support for the idea that the end justifies the means is found in attempts to rework the tradition. Here, the ideologist argues that when "correctly" interpreted the tradition justifies certain apparent violations of the normative order. Heinrich von Treitschke's effort to square Christianity with aggressive war is an excellent example of this tactic. Treitschke lays his groundwork by asserting that Christianity has no moral code: "The chief commands of Christianity are love and liberty for conscience. A moral code is exactly what is lacking, and therein its very morality lies."[7] Having reduced the tradition to its minimal principles, Treitschke argues that since Schleiermacher it has been universally recognized that the way of putting these principles into practice is for every Christian "to know himself, to develop his personality and act in accordance with it."[8] Particularly, whoever is an artist "and knows it" has "the right to develop his gift before all else, and may put other duties in the background." [9] This standard of "deeper and truly Christian ethics" may be applied to the state. Since the "very personality" of the state is power, "its highest moral duty is to uphold that power." [10] Treitschke provides a morality for the state: "The injunction to assert itself remains always absolute. Weakness must always be condemned as the most disastrous and despicable of crimes, the unforgivable sin of politics." [11] In this way, Christianity itself has been put to work as a support for the double-moralities characteristic of expansionist justifications of violence. The end of self-realization, applied to an inanimate, legalistic entity, comes to justify any means.

Civilizing Mission

Beyond the double-morality, which merely carries the claim that since one's group is superior to others, members of other groups need not be treated with the same consideration due to members of one's own group, is the idea that one's own group has a civilizing mission with respect to other groups. This civilizing mission involves the notion that one's own group has the *duty* to impose its normative order on other peoples. Since the others may not see the advantage of this imposition immediately, they must be forced to take advantage of tutelage.

The view that some peoples have a civilizing mission became widespread in the nineteenth century as a justification for imperialism. The general pattern of this view can be grasped by examining the way in which the American sociologist, Franklin Henry Giddings, justified the Spanish-American War— "the task of governing from a distance the inferior races of mankind will be one of great difficulty—one that will tax every resource of intellect and character, but it is one that must be faced and overcome, if the civilized world is not to abandon all hope of continuing its economic conquest of the natural resources of the globe." [12] For Giddings and many other supporters of imperialism the "white man's burden" was ostensibly a moral obligation, not an opportunity for spoliation.

Of course, the expansionist's mode of justifying violence does not have to embrace the idea of a civilizing mission. The group against which violence is done may be deemed so inferior that it is only fit to be exploited and to serve as menial labor for the members of the group claiming superiority. Chattel slavery of blacks in the United States was frequently justified in this way. Further, the group against which violence is done may be deemed an evil and corrupting influence whose members should be exiled or exterminated. Perhaps the group is not so much regarded as "inferior" as it is deemed (perhaps implicitly) "dangerous," although the two adjectives often go hand in hand and serve complementary purposes. The destruction of the Jews by Nazi

Germany was justified in this way. The extremes to which the expansionist's ideology can be taken show clearly that dehumanization of the enemy is a central aspect of this way of thinking.

Justifications of Violence

The major purpose of this book is to analyze the functions given to violence in political ideologies. The major justification of violence in the expansionist's ideology is that it functions to facilitate the domination of a superior group over an inferior group. Among the many problems of expansionist ideology is justifying the claim to group superiority. Sometimes this claim is made without any further support. In other instances it is grounded in supposed biological factors (racial), ability to govern (political), or achievements in civilization (cultural). However, the existence and utilization of supports do not constitute central issues in the present discussion. Once the claim for group superiority has been made, the legitimacy of violence against the inferior group remains an open question. Thus, the justification of violence can be held separate from the justification of superiority. In an expansionist's ideology violence against the inferior is justified as a right and in some instances even the duty of the superior.

Pervasive Violence

The simplest legitimist argument against violence was the blanket condemnation of violence. Violence, some legitimists held, never solved any problem. The simplest expansionist argument in support of violence is the blanket acceptance (not necessarily approval) of it as a universal fact of human existence and a way of getting things done. While the legitimist saw violence as senseless, the expansionist views it as the law of life.

Affirmations of the ubiquity of violence tend to be based on social Darwinism. The ideologist claims that human existence is a struggle in which only the fittest groups survive, although a precise definition of fitness is rarely offered. Walter Bagehot provides an example of this line of argument. He begins with the principle that in "every particular state of the world, those nations which are strongest tend to prevail over the others; and in certain marked peculiarities the strongest tend to be the best." [13] He continues that this is the kind of doctrine "with which, under the name of natural selection in physical science, we have become familiar, and, as every great scientific conception tends to advance its boundaries and to be of use in solving problems not thought of when it was started, so here, what was put forward for mere animal history may, with a change of form, but an identical essence, be applied to human history." [14]

For Bagehot there is no doubt that the struggle is initially military. "Civilization begins, because the beginning of civilization is military."[15] Bagehot believes that as civilization is perfected the arts of peace supplant those of war. However, as the great nations pass from imposed conformity to variability they must be careful to preserve their strength. Unless the military spirit is maintained the civilized nation "will be trodden out; it will have lost the savage virtues in getting the beginning of the civilized virtues; and the savage virtues which tend to war are the daily bread of human nature."[16] Thus, violence by the civilized against the savage is justified by the inevitability of struggle ("nature is red in tooth and claw"), the principle of natural selection ("survival of the fittest"), and the efficacy of might ("the beginning of civilization is military").

Blanket acceptance of violence has no more in its favor than blanket condemnation of violence. It is primarily a way of opening the door to more elaborate justifications of violence by those who claim superiority.

Violence and Nobility

Once the ideologist has accepted violence as the law of life it is a short step to justifying particular acts of violence in terms of their contribution to noble ends. If one believes that violence is inevitable, one need not consider how to abolish it from human affairs. Instead, the primary consideration is how to use it in the service of the good. Perhaps Treitschke carried this line of reasoning to its ultimate conclusion. Taking for granted the superiority of European, and particularly German, culture, he saw three alternatives for the peoples of the "tropics." These peoples could be exterminated, absorbed into the conquering race, or civilized. In the past, the struggle among nations had often led to extermination and/or absorption. Europeans would moralize this inevitable struggle: "The civilizing of a barbarian people is the best achievement."[17] In a clear example of expansionist thinking. Treitschke asserted: "The normal condition naturally is that the political victor should be in a position to impose his culture and manners upon the people he has subjugated."[18]

According to Treitschke violence is a necessary part of the civilizing mission. He begins his defense of violence by stating a moral postulate: "Whenever it is possible to attain an end which is moral in itself by methods which are also moral these should be preferred, even when they lead more slowly and more circuitously towards the goal."[19] Following from this principle is the idea that "the political methods of dealing with races upon a lower level of civilization must be adapted to their capacity for feeling and understanding."[20] Unfortunately, the capacity of these races is very low and "coercion by terror is necessary for self-preservation."[21] Thus, building on the foundation that violence is the law of life, Treitschke argues that violence in the service of a civilizing mission is a moral duty.

Violence to End Violence

A variation on the justification of violence as a means to performing a civilizing mission is the idea that violence used by the superior group will tend to minimize the total magnitude of violent incidents in the long run. This is the opposite of the legitimist claim that violence tends to bring on counterviolence in a never-ending chain, just as the claim that violence is an effective instrument in the civilizing mission is the opposite of the legitimist idea that violence is never creative. More than the other expressions of expansionist ideology, the idea of violence to minimize violence in the long run seems to be associated with a specific historical period, the era of Victorian optimism. Of course, the recent application of the domino theory to support American intervention in Southeast Asia may be a variant of this approach.

Walter Bagehot provides an illustration of the argument. In *Physics and Politics* he remarks that "the aggregate fighting power of mankind has grown immensely, and has been growing continuously since we knew anything about it."[22] This general growth has been accompanied by a concentration of the force in the civilized nations. This situation has led to the happy result that the civilized peoples need no longer fear a barbarian invasion: "The barbarians are no longer so much as vanquished competitors; they have ceased to compete at all."[23]

Violence in the Service of Freedom

Among the most interesting variations on the civilizing function of violence is the argument of Franklin Henry Giddings justifying the participation of the United States in the Spanish-American War. Here, violence is justified as a means to its antithesis, freedom. Giddings' argument is particularly important because it underlies many contemporary justifications of American military activites and, thus, provides some historical depth to current debates.

Giddings begins with the observation that because of the Puritan tradition in the United States neither the thirst for vengeance, the love of adventure, nor the desire for commercial opportunity could induce Americans to go to war. Americans will fight a war only if they can "find a pretext" that appeals "either to their sympathies or to their sense of justice."[24] However, such pretexts mask the real justifications for the Spanish-American War: "Are world politics to be dominated by English-speaking people in the interest of an English civilization, with its principles of freedom, self-government, and opportunity for all; or by the Russian-Chinese combination, with its policy of exclusiveness and its tradition of irresponsible authority?"[25] Giddings concludes with a challenge to American responsibility: "The victory of Chalons forever turned back the hordes of Asian barbarism from their westward advance. Were they stopped in their eastward advance by the guns of Admiral Dewey's fleet? It is for the people of the United States to say."[26] Thus, the final twist of missionary's consciousness is the idea of the war to impose a normative order based on freedom. As will be demonstrated shortly, the notion of such a "civilizing" mission is still very much alive today.

Instability of Expansionist Ideologies

Justifications of violence based on the alleged superiority of a group arise in a situation of competing normative orders. When there is such competition violence is often used to impose one of the normative orders. Justifications for such violence build upon the proposition that violence is a normal part of human existence. Once this proposition has been accepted it becomes a matter of deciding how best to use violence. Since the law of life is survival of the fittest, there is a duty of the more advanced peoples to maintain their supremacy over the barbarians. In maintaining that supremacy they are expected to perform a civilizing mission.

There is an ambiguity at the core of expansionist ideologies. At first, it appears that this view advocates using might as a means to promoting a superior normative order. However, given the acceptance of the universal struggle to survive, the only measure of superiority is greater might. Thus, might becomes the only measure of right. It is a short step from this position to the stance that might is right. Treitschke's idea that power is the essence of the state becomes the notion that power is the greatest political good.

Treitschke

The ambiguity in expansionist ideologies of violence is most apparent in the work of Heinrich von Treitschke, the writer who expressed most completely the content of the expansionist's mode. Treitschke's revision of Christianity and his defense of the civilizing mission have already been discussed. In these two discussions the tension between might and right is clearly present. In his revision of Christianity, Treitschke argues that the essence of the state is power. Its role in the world is to maintain and expand that power. Thus, might and right seem to be identified. However, in the defense of the civilizing mission Treitschke claims that moral methods are preferred "even when they lead more slowly and more circuitously towards the goal." Here, right seems to be independent of might.

It is not the purpose of the present discussion to resolve this ambiguity in expansionist ideologies, if such a resolution is possible. Instead, the aim is to consider briefly the justification of violence based on the idea that superior power itself is the highest political good. This is the justification called upon when all others fail.

Treitschke begins his defense by defining the state as power: "Since the State is power, it can obviously draw all human action within its scope, so long as that action arises from the will which regulates the outer lives of men, and belongs to their visible common existence."[27] As ultimate arbiter of all action, the state makes the triumph over barbarism actual through the sword. War is also justified between civilized nations because it is the form of litigating disputes between states. War brings unintended benefits in its train. It unites nations, because through combat opponents "learn to know and to respect each other's peculiar qualities."[28] The greatest benefits of war, however, accrue directly to the nation. Social selfishness and party hatreds "must be dumb before the call of the State when its existence is at stake."[29] War brings out nobility and is the most effective way of transporting human beings beyond their own selfish desires and into the realm of morality: "The grandeur of war lies in the utter annihilation of puny man in the great conception of the State, and it brings out the full magnificence of the sacrifice of fellow-countrymen for one another." [30]

From the preceding discussion of the direct benefits of violence, Treitschke passes on to an argument that power is a good in itself. He states that all judgments of public morality "must be based on the hypothesis of the State as power, constrained to maintain itself as such within and without, and of man's highest, noblest destiny being co-operation in this duty."[31] Here, power itself becomes the mark of superiority and might is indissolubly linked to right. This is not Treitschke's usual position, but it shows the extensions of expansionist thought. Expansionist justifications of violence begin with the idea that violence is ubiquitous, move on to the notion that violence is justified as a means to civilization, and end with the claim that violence is justified as a mark and a demonstration of power. In the final analysis, might does not make right; it *is* right.

Given the concern with power for its own sake, the expansionist is caught in an embarrassing position with respect to revolution. If might is right a successful revolution would appear to be right. Despite his high regard for the state Treitschke defends some revolutions. He notes that in his perspective revolution and legitimacy are relative to one another: "the two expressions, legitimacy and revolution, are elastic. A lawful development is the normal, but to every State without exception moments arrive when it can go no further upon peaceful lines, and war without or revolution within becomes inevitable." [32] With this statement Treitschke is beyond ideology. He has become the utilitarian *par excellence*. He is committed to defending anyone who is successful in seizing and holding power. He is neither defending nor attacking a normative order.

Heinrich von Treitschke was merely the most articulate and complete defender of violence among many European and American thinkers of the late nineteenth and early twentieth centuries. His work is unique in that it is not primarily concerned with justifying the claim to group superiority.

Treitschke took for granted the superiority of the German culture and devoted himself to justifying the use of violence as a means to its triumph. In his effort he elaborated themes which would be taken up by both dictatorships and democracies in the twentieth century. Among these themes were violence as a civilizing instrument, violence as a moralizing force in the nation, and power as an end in itself. Treitschke never resolved the ambiguity between power as a means to civilization and power as a measure of civilization. This ambiguity has remained to haunt the expansionist ideology.

Contemporary Expansionism

In its practical application, the expansionist's consciousness has assumed multiple contours. It has become most familiar to us in the pontifications of the nineteenth century European powers as they strained to convince themselves and others of the rectitude of their scramble for colonies. It is no less alive, though usually in disguised and often self-deluded forms, today. Missionaries and expansionists are no longer in vogue. In twentieth century liberal America and Europe the expansionist rationalizations for the use of force and violence have been discredited, at least in all but the eyes of the users. This is not to say, however, that they are not employed as the situation demands. But blatant utterances are more difficult to find.

The most characteristic contemporary expressions of the expansionist mode are in the foreign policies of the regimes that use the legitimist rationalization in the maintenance of the status quo at home. It is most applicable, not when a regime seeks to reinforce or reassert its dominance over peoples and territories to which it enjoys legitimate (that is, legal) claim, but when it seeks to extend its power and hegemony over people currently beyond its sway, or when the evolution of ideas has rendered control by outsiders over an indigenous population immoral or illegal. The expansionist ideology is then employed to justify the use of violence against peoples of a radically different culture or race, under the guise of preparing them to function in a "superior" system. Even within the confines of one territorial entity, the dominant order may use the expansionist mode to rationalize violence, provided the target is perceived to be sufficiently different, as defined by the dominant order. Thus various modes of thought on violence may be marshalled simultaneously by the same system. A confluence of ideas need not signify a confusion of purpose or an inconsistency of ideology when the very foundations of the order are in question. It merely points up the situational component in ideologies of violence.

Portugal

The ambiguity that puzzled Treitschke, between power as a means to civilization and power as a manifestation of civilization, does not bedevil present-day Portuguese ideologists when they mouth rationalizations for Portugal's continued and authoritarian presence in her "overseas provinces." In their eyes, power cannot be a measure of civilization since, in many ways, Portugal is fighting a rear-guard campaign against the winds of barbarian (i.e., communistic) change, or so they would have it. Rather, power is an instrument in the transmission of higher principles based upon a rebirth in the commitment to a species of natural law. That Portugal has fallen from her once great imperial heights may or may not be regrettable, but it does necessitate a departure from the power-equals-civilization persuasion. To be sure, Portuguese power *vis à vis* that of her African wards may currently be paramount. But the exigencies of international politics demand that she perceive her status in global, not simply provincial terms. Thus the support of her allies in NATO and in Southern Africa becomes not only an important instrument for successful Portuguese counter-insurgency but it is regarded, by Portuguese thinkers, as a type of testimonial to the values of Portuguese (read Christian and Western) civilization. Conversely, however, the growing strength and appeal of various nationalistic liberation movements and their expanding international contacts and supports cannot be regarded as a mark of their level of civilization.

Nor should we be misled by the definitional classification established in 1951 by Lisbon that relabelled her colonies "overseas provinces" and hence integral parts of metropolitan Portugal. Such legalistic pretensions have fooled few, particularly among those who live under the Portuguese regime. The legalisms are for the benefit of international law and to reduce pressures from the United Nations. At heart the old ideological motifs prevail. Occasionally one still finds references to a pre-nineteenth century rationalization of imperialism interspersed with a concentration on the theme of cultural superiority based upon a qualitative interpretation of natural law. Not unexpectedly, sometimes momentary, sometimes institutionalized self-delusion may grip Portugal or her individual leaders.

The thrust of the Portuguese rationalization for her presence in Africa is that the Portuguese nation is duty bound to colonize and transform Africa according to the natural and divine higher principles that have historically characterized Portuguese civilization. God is the font of all power. The Portuguese state is an instrument of God's will. In the words of the Archbishop of Lourenço Marques:

> This filial submission, due to the Fatherland, can only be demanded from us, in conscience, by our native Nation. But when it commands, adhering to the national and divine laws, we must obey, even if it compels us to leave home and go to the battle field.
>
> In fact, the Fatherland is one of the instruments used by God to rule individuals and families and that is why He confers on it a part of His supreme power.

These principles then are universal, immutable, constant. And they are embodied in Portuguese state policy, ostensibly one of "cultural integration and cultural interpenetration, and not the aggressive expansion of the dominant group."[34] Where Portuguese culture is imposed upon and displaces African forms, "it is merely in those fields in which the maintenance of human dignity demands a degree of intervention," all of which are putatively in keeping with various universal declarations of the Rights of Man. In Portuguese ideology, Portugal has always been committed to these principles, for on the grounds of "public order" it is her official duty to prevent "practices that are contrary to the morals and laws of mankind."[35] Not just the government of Portugal and the Portuguese nation, but the Church itself (as well as all corporate institutions within Portugal) are officially duty bound "to Christianize and educate, to nationalize and civilize" the African. Thus Portuguese imperialism, past and present, was no ordinary European imperialism. It did not result, so the official version goes, in exploitation, the oppression of a vanquished people, or the systematic exploitation of a people for Europe's aggrandizement. On the contrary, Portuguese imperialism is characterized by altruism, abnegation, faith, and an historic responsibility for civilization. To fulfill these responsibilities, undivided power is required. For if the native does not see or wish to achieve the blessings of Portuguese civilization, the state, the Church, and the nation must combine to impose civilization on the reluctant. "Our whole policy," wrote Morais Cabral, has been and continues to be to improve the cultural, economic, and social level of the Negro, to give him opportunities, to drag him from his ignorance and backwardness, to try to make of him a rational and honorable individual, worthy of the Lusitanian community."[36]

This expansionist mode is also embedded in the Portuguese Constitution. On the one hand, Article 8 (3) assures all Portuguese of the same individual guarantees, including "the freedom and inviolability of religious belief and practice." On the other hand, the Catholic religion is designated as the "religion of the Portuguese nation" (Article 45). A former Secretary of State for Overseas Administration sought to explicate this apparent inconsistency by arguing that this places a special burden on Catholics as a group "historically responsible for the creation of the Portuguese State as a whole." It is this "inequality of obligations" that he strives to emphasize rather than the unequal application of Portugal's native policics. "From the point of view of its constitutional preeminence, it seems clear to us [the Portuguese Government] that the original group responsible for the expansion has had a mission of public interest Overseas which appears in the greater intensity of its civic duties. The 'Missionary Statute' is the logical corollary of this fundamental premise."[37]

In the transmission process, the higher principles and natural laws alluded to are somehow invariably lost in their transference to Africa. The result is an exploitation no less repressive that that imposed by other colonial regimes. If Portugal herself has little material gain to show for her almost five-hundred years of empire it is not from a dedication to the betterment of indigenous peoples. Rather, this professed dedication became deflected early in her colonial history, deflected at first by a casual lack of interest in her overseas African territories, and later by her interests in retaining her African holdings and making them pay, at least for selected Portuguese groups and for the colonists themselves. By and large, it is simply for want of capital and efficient modes of management that Portugal was unable to enrich herself. The real tone of Portuguese colonial rule is exemplified by this statement by a former Colonial Minister:

> It is necessary to inspire in the black the idea of work and of abandoning his laziness and his depravity if we want to exercise a colonizing action to protect him.
>
> If vagrancy and crime in whites are punished, we cannot condone it in blacks. . . .if we scorn the white who lives on the work of a woman, we cannot permit the African to do the same.
>
> If we want to civilize the native we must make him adopt as an elementary moral precept the notion that he has no right to live without working.
>
> A productive society is based on painful hard work, obligatory even for vagrants, and we cannot permit any exception because of race.
>
> The policy of assimilation which I conceive of must be complete. Therefore it is necessary to establish a rule of conduct for the black which exists for the white, asking him to acquire a sense of responsibility. It is to be an unenlightened Negrophile not to infuse the African with the absolute necessity for work.[38]

Although the Protestant ethic never really permeated Portuguese society, it has been invoked and intermittently applied with a vengeance to her African wards. Running throughout these paragraphs is a tone of superiority and disdain for things African. The element of compulsion is thinly disguised, if at all. Against those who resist the imposition of the external order, or those who continue to maintain a self-respect and pride in themselves and their heritage and life-style, the use of violence is justified. After all, are they not resisting the dictates of a changeless, universal natural law? Not only must the superiority of the Portuguese order be demonstrated, by imposition if necessary, but the inferiority of African ways, though ostensibly self-evident, must be established to everyone's, particularly the African's, satisfaction. And this is undertaken with ruthless, though often incomplete and inefficient, determination.

A policy based upon an ideology of cultural superiority is not one based purely upon genotypical designations. On the contrary, genotype should be unimportant. At least such a philosophy maintains that members of the inferior cultural group deserve to be uplifted rather than exploited or exterminated. It holds out the hope that elements of the subject group may find acceptance in the superior culture.

Although a proselytizing assimilationist philosophy is theoretically not a racialist philosophy, in practice it often is. Even if the acceptance of a few converts into the controlling culture or even into its power structure represents a possible setback for the philosophy of racial arrogance, it also represents, in turn, a triumph of the philosophy of cultural arrogance. In interpersonal relations the convert knows that he now is no longer fully acceptable to either cultural group. He has been blinded by the promise of acceptance, yet psychologically as well as objectively he is unacceptable as a man without status in either community. Cultural arrogance, unless it makes good on *all* its commitments, may well be more pernicious than racial arrogance. It functions under the pretense that it is not discriminatory and arbitrary, and that it is willing to admit of some social change. Although imitation may be regarded as the highest form of flattery, it is to a degree also a tacit admission of cultural inferiority by the convert. The principle of assimilation might possibly be efficacious when applied to a minority group divorced from its roots being assimilated into the dominant, truly open majority group. But when a superordinate minority insists that the majority must adopt its culture (as in Portuguese Africa at its theoretical best) and, moreover, refuses to provide the vast majority with opportunities to adapt, then the integrity of the missionary's commitment is questionable. This is especially so when coercion is substituted for opportunity and genuine sympathetic encouragement. In these cases, expansionist ideology simply reflects a recognition by forces of the status quo that it is strategically less disruptive to comply symbolically by admitting or cultivating a few "Europeanized" blacks into white institutions than it would be to resist uncompromisingly by fighting to the bitter end. If one can "disarm" the forces of change, violence can be made a less important component of the status quo. Even if assimilated fully into a European culture, for what it is worth, such natives would be little more than exhibits, tokens, and refugees from an "inferior" culture. Thus the expansionist mode never really comes to grips with the problem of racial and cultural diversity.

The Vietnam War

A more extreme manifestation of the expansionist rationalization for violence would be one in which it is held that the "inferior" targets of the "superior" culture do not even possess the potentiality for achieving civilization and uplift. Usually such attitudes revert to racist slogans, although occasionally the expansionist mode will find expression in the policy that it is noble to "protect" these people (invariably from some more ruthless or exploitative outsiders) by organizing them to sustain and support the dominant society. Thus they become instruments, tools, slaves to continued foreign rule. A modern corollary might be the use of them as mercenaries in the defense of the superior culture.

An element of this mentality may from time to time have crept into the policy of Vietnamization of the Indochinese war. Thus the "savage virtues" that Bagehot wrote of enabled the United States to use the "gooks" to prevent the domino collapse of Southeast Asia, which was, in turn, thought to be bound up with the defense of the United States itself. Granted, nowhere can such an expansionist viewpoint be found in official U.S. ideology in Vietnam. But one cannot help but see reflections of this in the attitudes of many of the officers and men who served in Vietnam. The massacre of My Lai is but a single manifestation of a polar expression of this mentality. The tensions and frustrations of counterinsurgency notwithstanding, this could not have happened had not a mental transformation occured, by which the Vietnamese became, in the eyes of some of the men, subspecies. Erik Erikson called it "pseudospeciation." Americans began to think of the South Vietnamese as sub-human or non-human, and thus apt targets for inhuman treatment or extermination. It is not an uncommon frame of reference for some people in Anglo-Saxon cultures, especially under the pressures and tensions of war.

What makes this an expansionist consciousness and not unadulterated racism is the intriguing fact that American fighting men in Southeast Asia did display a high respect for the courage, determination, ingenuity, and skill of the Viet Cong and the soldiers of North Vietnam. The irony is that, in many ways, for the instruments of culture contact and transformation—the U.S. fighting man—the enemy served as a model of manhood and cultural superiority, at least as that model applied to the Indochinese war.[39] These qualities were felt to prevail in regard to the fighting skills of the enemy. Nevertheless, the uplifting expansionist philolphy *vis à vis* Southeast Asia still was at the root of official behavior. It was accepted by policy-makers that self-determination, as defined and operationalized by Washington, was best for South Vietnam. Since the Vietnamese war was an event external to the United States, since the enemy had initiated hostilities and chosen the medium of conflict, and since "war is hell" (which is often used to justify the use of violence as much as to decry it), those responsible for starting it should be taught a lesson. The will to punish wrongdoers and the justice of retribution are very much a part of the expansionist mentality. This, then, represents the efficacy of violence, and its blindness as well.

Expansionism in Domestic Affairs

Both of the examples mentioned above, the Portuguese in Africa and the United States in Indochina, pertain to the expansionists's rationalization for violence in the context of societies in territories external to the dominant regime. A foreign or colonial policy enables a regime to indulge in behavior that would be difficult if not impossible to sanction in a domestic situation. To the attentive public it may actually test the legitimacy of the regime itself. Still, there are cases where the expansionist ideology is invoked to countenance violent behavior against inhabitants of the same territory. It is to such "Domestic mission" that we shall now turn.

In states that are composed of multifarious peoples, arrangements must be worked out for the peaceable maintenance and continuity of the system. So goes the view of those segments of the population that seek unity and strength for the state, as it has been constituted. Particularly in many of the newly independent states, where national boundaries had been established by colonial powers with little concern for the prevailing patterns of social homogeneity of the indigenous peoples and where the experience of living together has been relatively brief, schismatic tendencies are the daily stuff of politics. The central government, then, may be faced with a constant struggle to maintain the integrity of the state, its subordinate institutions, and its ancillary expressions. The magnitude and form of violence in the system then depends, *inter alia*, on the intensity and extent of such fissiparous forces, and the determination and ability of the central government to mollify, transcend, eliminate, or replace them. By and large, the response of the regime is usually a form of the legitimist justification for the use of violence as developed in chapter two. But if societal divisions are deep, and cultural distinctions are sufficiently obvious to the relevant actors, the dominant regime may reason that the only long range solution to the problems of internal disorder and instability is to remove the causes of endemic discontent by bridging by force the cultural distinctions that contribute to conflicting perspectives and hence, to political and social dissension. From the perspective of the dissidents, however, it is the repressive use of coercion by the central government that is responsible for domestic conflict. Almost mirror images by dissident leaders in two neighboring African states illustrate this point. The leader of the Chad National Liberation Front (FROLINAT), an essentially northern and Muslim-based revolutionary movement, claims that:

> The present head of state has practiced a policy of discrimination and systematic oppression towards the Muslim half of the country. All important posts are handed to Southerners, who committed blunder after blunder and exaction after exaction. The civil servants of southern origin who took over the administration in the north after independence were in no way trained for their task and they rapidly came to be detested.[40]

One southern Sudanese leader puts it less forcefully by not making the case for exploitation. But by essentially ruling out any sense of shared future with

the central government in Khartoum, there is no less a sting in his description of Sudanese social problems.

> The Sudan falls sharply into two distinct areas, both in geographical area, eth-
> nic group, and cultural systems, The Northern Sudan is occupied by a hybrid
> Arab race who are united by their common language, common culture, and
> common religion; and they look to the Arab world for their cultural and politi-
> cal inspiration. The people of the Southern Sudan, on the other hand, belong to
> the African ethnic group of East Africa. They do not only differ from the hy-
> brid Arab race in origin, arrangement and basic systems, but in all conceivable
> purposes .... There is nothing in common between the various sections of the
> community; no body of shared beliefs, no identity of interests, no local signs of
> unity and above all, the Sudan has failed to compose a single community.[41]

Here, then, we have a northern Muslim in Chad accusing a southern black
government of subjugating his people, and a southern black in the Sudan
documenting what he regards as unbridgeable cultural and racial distinctions and, by implication, calling for political separation and an end to domination by one group over another.

Not only is there a sociocultural separation in the Sudan, but secessionist
leaders would maintain that the regime has consciously sought to exploit that
cleavage at the same time that it sought to overcome the hiatus by imposing
an Arabicized culture on the southern provinces. If we can believe the seces-
sionists, and there is a good deal of evidence to document their case, the expansionist mode had a contemporary champion in the Sudanese central government.[42] In other words, the government sought to enforce unity in the
Sudan by Arabicizing the peoples and institutions of the south, at the same
time admitting that some constitutional safeguards might be negotiable. After
independence, the Khartoum government attempted to Sudanize the south,
and especially its educational system, by introducing Arabic instruction,
new curricula, and Arab teachers. Although northerners insisted that they
were trying to raise standards, southerners charged them with "cultural imperialism." One southern leader stated that "Imperialists do not always
come from overseas and are not always white. We lost our freedom when we
gained our independence." Nevertheless, a good case can be made that the
Arabic culture did provide the cement for unifying the once diverse peoples of
the northern Sudan. Integration in the north had been achieved at least in the
sense of a perceived national identity. Why not a similar process in the eco-
nomically retarded south? If the south is going to be modernized and traditional ways are to be changed, why not change them in a direction that would
render greater homogenity with the Arab north? Be that as it may, the reasoning is still akin to expansionist thinking, for the process is not a harmonious cultural amalgamation but rather a cultural transference. Domestic colonialism prevails, albeit under the guise of a (we must assume) perfectly

sincere effort at national integration. Meanwhile, the repression and violent reprisals have served to divide the country even more. Even the present reconciliation, of sorts, has yielded an ominous and uneasy calm, containing all the ingredients for another eruption.

If the threat to the regime is regarded as marginal, or if the potential contribution to national values (be they development, unity, power, or some such nebulous norms) of the non-integrated peoples is not felt to be vital, then the regime may simply ignore or isolate the problem. Brazil has done this regarding the Indians of the upper Amazon. Thus the regime may do nothing and regard the source of the difference insignificant or as a healthy cultural diversity until such time as it may want to reorder the relationships. If, however, the divisive threat is sufficiently imposing, especially if it is associated with valuable or strategically important territory, then force may be employed, and the justification may well reflect an expansionist's attitude toward violence.

What we have called a "domestic mission" is not new. Moreover, it or something similar (such as "domestic colonialism") are not the epithets applied by the regime. Rather, they are more commonly used by the anti-systemic forces. For example, a Bengali leader before the independence of Bangladesh had stated: "We have never been anything but a colony of the west [Pakistan]."[43] Today, colonialism is a perjorative term, since it reeks of super- and subordination in an era of popular egalitarianism. As governments embark on such homogenizing schemes calling them anything they will, they would, of course, prefer to eschew violence. If voluntary compliance or emulation could be assured this phenomenon would not be a fit subject for this study. But volition is a rare commodity in intercultural political relations. Consequently, recalcitrant groups are coerced in an effort to make them identify with the regime or at least with the state, and to abandon their traditional or distinctive ways. The government rationalizes this behavior by claiming that it is striving to create national or class consciousness, which after all are "modern" phenomena, or to establish the foundation for economic development and hence for reducing economic disparities, or to reduce the likelihood of neo-colonialist penetration by eliminating dissenting linkage groups that would provide entry for external interests. The specific motives of those participating in violence justified by an expansionist ideology may be diverse—moral, racial, ethnic, religious, economic, political, or some combination of these. Thus, in the Sudan, it is commonplace to hear a northerners refer to a southerner as *abaid* (slave). Governments, of course, would never openly subscribe to this mentality. Rare candor was demonstrated by one Pakistani army major during the Bangladesh war of independence. After the soldiers practically destroyed Dacca University, this military man reportedly said:

We have to consider that an entire generation of students has been lost, because of the laxity and permissiveness of parents. You hear of alcohol drinking and raping going on at the university—things unheard of in a Moslem society. People like that become miscreants inevitably. They end by taking up arms and getting shot by us. The new generation must be brought up according to strict Islamic principles, with a return to the old ways. Too many people forget that the sole reason for the existence of Pakistan is as a home for Moslems. When we lose sight of that idea, we become corrupt.[44]

The "miscreants" and "anti-social elements" become fitting targets for regime violence, and conversely, it could be said that those who become targets for regime violence are, by definition, "miscreants." But for outside consumption, the expansionist rationalization seems to be all the present-day market will bear. It is uncanny how higher principles have a habit of taking on a distinctly parochial coloration in concrete application. In an era of the increasing expression of micro-nationalisms and the desire for more intimate group identities we can expect a reappearance of the expansionist's mentality on both sides, but especially among those who seek to make national consciousness coterminous with state boundaries.

We have seen how expansionist thought patterns become a central feature of certain types of violent behavior. By appealing to higher values, baser behavior may be legitimized. Hence, ambiguity and doctrinal dilemma are not unique with legitimist modes. They have been institutionalized and routinized within the expansionist rationalization for violence.

Examples of the expansionist's justification for violence, though they may have reached their apogee in the nineteenth century Victorian "scramble for Africa" and in imperialist expressions of Christian, Anglo-Saxon and Teutonic superiority, have displayed surprising longevity and adaptability in contemporary inter-cultural relations. Often repeated phrases and code words became magic incantations which made practically any nefarious behavior right and necessary. Writers like Paul Leroy-Beaulieu, Sir John R. Seeley, and Rudyard Kipling may have popularized the expansionist mentality amongst the peoples of Europe's dominant colonial powers, but it is Kipling's "sullen peoples," not all, but some, who today as leaders of independent governments are no less inclined to be at home with the message of his rhythmic verse.

This transformed locus for the acceptance of the expansionist mode in domestic affairs may be little more than a product of historical timing. The Western world has long since effected the intersection of state and nation, generally speaking, although recent trends indicate a regeneration of the questions of national homogeneity. The Communist world possesses a different ideological basis for its coercive behavior, although nationalism has captivated its peoples and displayed a durability that has proven to be a challenge for various Party theoreticians. The extensive colonial empires of the early twentieth century have been shrunken and their ideological underpinnings have been eroded. Into this situation are placed states that recently gained their sovereignty and formal independence from the colonial powers. But these states are rarely a harmonious blend of indigenous peoples. They have not as yet generated a distillation of and commitment to a single national consciousness. Territorial designations have not been adjusted to dissolve and mollify conflicting internal identities. Hence there is greater need for an ideology capable of rationalizing and justifying the use of violence in hammering together viable and relatively permanent political entities. Enter, among others, the expansionist banner, carried by the new governing elites anxious for a doctrine that can mesmerize and inspire their peoples to cooperative sacrifice and effort. But such inspirational codes for one group may yield an equally intent and dedicated resistance from other quarters within the divergent state. The result is the instability that has marked the nation-building, or in stronger terms, the assimilation process thus far. The expansionist ideology may grow out of the situational conditions that today are most commonly found in the Third World. Insofar as it proves helpful in dealing with the challenges of state management and nation building it will survive as a domestic political ideology.

The temper of the times does not permit the deliberate and overt appeal to blatant racist ideology or to policies based upon openly assumed cultural or racial superiority. Moreover, in the day to day struggle for political predominance and order users may not realize the underlying nature of their appeals and motivations. This does not mean that such appeals and policies no longer exist. It means only that the old expansionist mode must be muted, more subtle, less visible, and that policy pronouncement be designed to deceive as much as to communicate. That being the case, although it is more difficult to detect contemporary public expressions of expansionist ideology, actual political behavior is, as it always should be, the best index of ideological predisposition.

Notes

1. Francis W. Coker, *Recent Political Thought* (New York: D. Appleton-Century Company, 1934), p. 456.

2. Ibid., p. 456.

3. Ibid., p. 457.

4. William Ernest Hocking, *Strength of Men and Nations* (New York: Harper and Bros. 1958), p. 68.

5. Ibid., p. 70.

6. Ibid., p. 68.

7. Heinrich von Treitschke, *Politics*, Vol. I (New York: The Macmillan Company, 1916),

p. 93. The concept of the "just war" which runs throughout Christian, that is, church philosophy, justifies the use of violence, usually on different grounds. See Roland H. Bainton, *Christian Attitudes Toward War and Peace* (New York: Abingdon, 1960).

8. Ibid, p. 93.

9. Ibid., p. 94.

10. Ibid., p. 94.

11. Ibid., pp. 94-95.

12. Franklin Henry Giddings, *Democracy and Empire* (New York: The Macmillan Company, 1901), pp. 284-85. The practical implications of these views are discussed in *The Clash of Cultures: Early Race Relations in Central Africa* (New York: Frederick A. Praeger, 1965).

13. Walter Bagehot, *Physics and Politics* (Boston: Beacon Press, 1956), p. 32. For an imaginative treatment of the evolution of social Darwinism see Ali A. Mazrui, "From Social Darwinism to Current Theories of Modernization: A Tradition of Analysis," *World Politics* 21 (October 1968).

14. Bagehot, *Physics and Politics*, p. 33.

15. Ibid., p. 39.

16. Ibid., p. 45.

17. Treitschke, *Politics*, p. 121.

18. Ibid., p. 121.

19. Ibid., p. 99.

20. Ibid., p. 100.

21. Ibid., p. 100.

22. Bagehot, *Physics and Politics*, p. 34.

23. Ibid., p. 35.

24. Giddings, *Democracy and Empire*, p. 278.

25. Ibid., p. 289.

26. Ibid., p. 290.

27. Treitschke, *Politics*, p. 62.

28. Ibid., p. 66.

29. Ibid., pp. 66-67.

30. Ibid., p. 65.

31. Ibid., p. 99.

32. Ibid., pp. 129-30.

33. Dom Teodósio Clemente de Gouveia, *The Voice of the Pastor* (Lisbon: Agência Geral do Ultramar, 1961), p. 12.

34. Adriano Moreira, *Political Unity and the Status of Peoples* (Lisbon: Agência Geral do Ultramar, 1960), pp. 31-32.

35. Ibid., p. 32.

36. As quoted in James Duffy, *Portuguese Africa* (Cambridge, Mass.: Harvard University Press, 1959), p. 292.

37. Moreira, *Political Unity*, pp. 18-19.

38. As quoted in Duffy, *Portuguese Africa*, p. 318.

39. Charles J. Levy, "ARVN as Faggots: Inverted-Warfare in Vietnam," *Trans-action* 7 (October 1971): 18-27.

40. Dr. Abba Siddick as quoted in Robert Pledge, "France at War in Africa," *Africa Report* 15 (June 1970): 17.

41. Aggrey Jaden as quoted in: George W. Shepherd, Jr., "National Integration and the

Southern Sudan," *Journal of Modern African Studies* 4 (October 1966): 195.

42. The southern case is well argued in: Oliver Albino, *The Sudan: A Southern Viewpoint* (London: Oxford University Press, 1970). A book more sympathetic to the government is M. O. Beshir, *The Southern Sudan: Background to Conflict* (London: G. Hurst & Co., 1967). An essay dealing with the ramifications of these issues is Ali A. Mazrui, "The Multiple Marginality of the Sudan," in his *Violence and Thought: Essays on Social Tensions in Africa* (London: Longman, 1969), pp. 163-83.

43. "Bengal: The Murder of a People," *Newsweek*, 2 August 1971, pp. 26-27.

44. As quoted in the *New York Times*, 13 May 1971, p. 3.

Chapter Four

Pluralist Ideologies of Violence

The hallmark of the modern modes of consciousness is sharp awareness of alternative and often competing normative orders. Expansionist ideologies of violence respond to this diversity by declaring that one out of the many normative orders is superior to the others. Thus, the expansionist mentality justifies political violence by arguing that it is committed in the service of extending the favored order. The *pluralist* justification for violence comes essentially as a response to expansionist thinking. In its most fully developed form, pluralism may declare that no one normative order is intrinsically superior to any other. Each group has its own particular design for living, which is adapted to its specific needs. This means that pluralism brands as illegitimate any attempt to impose an alien normative order on a group of people. While it deplores the use of violence to impose an order, it justifies violence committed in the service of self-determination by groups seeking liberation from an imposed order. Thus, like the modes of consciousness already discussed, pluralist ideology justifies some acts of violence while condemning others. The problem is particularly acute here, because disadvantaged groups must often commit more visible acts of violence in pressing their claims than established elites commit in defending their privileges. This problem gives rise to a wide variety of variations on the theme of self-determination in the ideologies based upon pluralist thinking.

Probably the most popular justification of violence associated with this ideological mode is the simple claim that violence in the service of movements for self-determination is somehow inevitable. Applying this line of argument to defend campus protest against the Vietnam War, Kingsley Widmer contends: "all our violences can only be understood as part of the same psychological and ideological fabric [responsible for governmental violence]. Our protest did not arbitrarily choose violence; it was driven to it by an unresponsive order parading as 'moderation' and by the arrogant coercion which characterizes the American Second Empire style." [1] The phrase "driven to" in the preceding statement is ambiguous. Does it mean that the violence of campus protesters was somehow caused by the "unresponsive order"? Does it mean that their violence is understandable in the light of a supposedly desperate situation? Does it mean that the protestors took the only morally justifiable course of action considering the "arrogant coercion" of the government? It is easy to slip from one of these meanings to the next. This is the "scientific" style of argument in which the ideologist predicts that as long as certain supposedly oppressive social conditions continue, violence committed by the dispossessed group is inevitable. This claim is similar to the legitimist argument that violence inevitably breeds new waves of violence and the expansionist argument that violence is the law of life. None of these contentions is demonstrable *a priori*.

If the scientific style proves inadequate it is likely that the ideologist will appeal to sympathy. With regard to campus violence, he contends that since "violence, for no matter what ends, is rarely a just and effective social instrument, a reasonable and humane man cannot argue for it." [2] However, he adds that "it is much less often noted that we must not condemn such violence as that of protest on the ground that we cannot wisely condone it, any more than we can conclude that we must hate all those whom we cannot love." [3] The argument here is that although violence of dissenting groups cannot be condoned, it can at least be understood as the result of desperation and may even deserve a certain amount of sympathy. Thus, while one may not agree that the protester's choice to engage in violence was morally right, one can appreciate the reasons for this choice and perhaps argue that is was morally permissible.

The arguments that violence of dispossessed groups is inevitable and/or understandable are directed primarily at those who are not members of these groups. The inevitability argument functions as a threat or a warning to dominant groups and is aimed at gaining rectification of social conditions. It may also serve as a bid to escape punishment for acts of violence already committed. Both of these arguments employ Bentley's "is" and "must," and are best considered as attempts to gain outside support or at least benevolent neutrality for the group. Of course, they also provide rationalizations for the activities of certain members of the dispossessed groups.

When appeals to inevitability or sympathy seem to be inadequate, the ideologist is likely to argue that violence in the service of self-determination is morally justified. Such claims are at the center of pluralist reasoning.

Natural Law and the Justification of Violence

While the pluralist ideologies are a response to the imposition of a rejected normative order, they grow from legitimist roots. While legitimist justifications are normally used to defend an existing set of institutions, they can be turned around to justify violence aimed at restoring or instituting a normative order deemed universal. Thus, legitimist consciousness, particularly the tradition of Catholic natural law, contains justifications of violence aimed at rectifying social injustices. These justifications have been widely employed in the contemporary world, even though it is likely that definitions of justice vary widely within and between groups.

Martin J. Hillenbrand summarizes the central claim of the natural law justification of violence against established authority: "Only to prevent otherwise inevitable greater evil, physical or moral, in a case of conflict of rights, is the use of violence at all justifiable." [4] Applying this principle, Robert J. McNamara has attempted to defend some of the political violence committed by blacks in the United States. Extending the idea of just war to inter-group relations, McNamara argues that violence is justified when there is an aggressor and a victim, when other means of remedying the situation have failed and violence seems to have a good chance of success, and when the evil consequent to the acts of violence is less than the sought-for good. [5] Ernest W. Ranly has noted that these conditions for just war were first applied to domestic politics by John Locke. [6] Direct application of the principles to political revolutions has been made by Peter J. Riga: "the essential question is not one of violence or nonviolence, but of the radical change of power from a small, self-serving group of men to the people who will thus be enabled to shape their own destinies." [7] Riga's argument goes a step beyond the legitimist justification of violence by making the drive for self-determination a legitimate ground for violence. Some Protestant theologians have carried this argument even further. A committee of the World Council of Churches maintained that the use of physical force by dispossessed groups against the "systemic violence" (social and economic exploitation) of elites can be justified. It argued: "The question emerges today whether the violence which sheds blood in planned revolutions may not be a lesser evil than the violence which (though bloodless) condemns whole populations to perennial despair." [8] It concluded that violence aimed at redressing wrongs can be justified and that "Christians can insist that violent reactions to systemic violence demand massive understanding and drastic remedial programs rather than brutal reprisals." [9] Similarly mixing the appeal to sympathy with natural law, the Catholic Frederick D. Webber has argued: "When those in power can violate the law without disturbing the serene atmosphere of public order, the frustration of those out of power becomes so intense that violence is a natural result." [10]

The justifications of violence committed by the dispossessed presented above are pre-modern in the sense that they assume a given normative order to be natural. However, they easily slip into the pluralist mode by making self-determination a legitimate ground for violence. Natural law justifications of violence against established authority present peculiar problems in the contemporary world. Where there is a single widely accepted normative order, the relatively abstract principles defining a just war are likely to have relatively unambiguous applications to concrete situations. However, where there are alternative and often competing normative orders, there is likely to be wide variation in the applications of these principles to specific cases. Under these conditions the appeal to natural law loses some of its former efficacy. It often becomes a veil for the pursuit of highly particularized interests. This leads to the development of justifications of violence which are clearly modern in their recognition of cultural diversity.

Violence and the Clash of Interests

With the decline of natural law, justifications of violence arose based on more empirical standards. In this type of argument violence is justified when an important interest of a group has not been satisfied due to the opposition of one or more other groups. This kind of justification is usually undergirded by relativistic morality.

Professor Eliseo Vivas has presented an elaborate argument justifying violence from the perspective of pluralist ideology. He begins with a repudiation of natural law: "Empiricism in ethics has tended to the conclusion that morality obtains only within members of a group that somehow have found a basis for agreement, but that failure to find such a basis is outside the scope of morality." [11] Thus, morality itself is the result of a process of bargaining which may include the use of force: "force cannot only not be excluded from moral practice but must be admitted as a normal and intrinsic constituent of it." [12] This observation that force is normal, however, does not lead Vivas to glorify violence or to equate it with civilization as exponents of expansionism sometimes did. Instead, though he argues that "in a normally running society conflicts of forces are always present" and that "morality is an organization of forces," he concludes that "'right' is a term which is applied to a situation in which an organization of forces has been accomplished; i.e., in which a dynamic equilibrium exists between complex forces." [13] Thus, a social situation is "right" only to the degree in which such a dynamic equilibrium has been achieved. Someone who is not a party to a given political conflict will see wrong on the part of insurgents because they are disrupting an established equilibrium and wrong on the part of the conservatives because they are blocking satisfaction of new interests. When there are particularly violent disruptions, one can expect to find strong and persistent emergent interests and intransigeant established interests. While such disruptions indicate the "maximum of immorality," violence "is often the only means to which we can have recourse in order to effect a needed reorganization."[14] Since there is no authoritative standard for defining the content of the good life, the moral life becomes "an enterprise, a cooperative affair, a matter of adjusting stresses and giving play to strains, a form of living to be discovered and to be realized." [15] Within this process of give and take, conflict resolution can be accomplished through means ranging from discussion through war. While discussion is the preferable method, war is to be expected when emergent interests are blocked from satisfaction.

Justifications of violence based on moral relativism have a serious weakness from the ideologist's viewpoint. The most that the ideologist can say is that the violence of the group that he is defending is just as legitimate as the violence of the established group. He can attempt to claim that such violence is "inevitable" because "strong and persistent" interests have been denied, or that the violence of the dispossessed is "understandable" in the light of their frustration, but he cannot argue that the interests of the dispossessed are any more legitimate than those of the established group. It remains up to each individual to determine which group he will support. This ideological weakness is related to an important feature of moral relativism. Moral relativists are committed to suspending judgment on the goodness of the content of any particular interest. This means that they cannot consistently condemn interests in war or any other form of violence for its own sake, or interests in harming another group for its own sake. Moreover, they cannot consistently condemn interests by their very nature contradictory to the establishment of a "dynamic equilibrium" of interests. In other words, they are logically bound to treat their preferences for peaceful conflict resolution and wide harmonies of interest as relative to all other interests. In practice, of course, they usually fail to do this, and argue that the interest in self- determination takes precedence over interests in domination. However, while there is nothing to stop the ideologist from doing this, it leaves his position exposed to the attacks of adversaries. When he treats all interests as equal, the pluralist loses the self-confidence and certainty which are the hallmarks of the legitimist and expansionist positions.

The problem in the pluralist justification of violence becomes particularly acute in constitutional democracies. In such regimes defenders of the *status quo* argue that violence is not justified because there is an operative process through which demands for change can be channelled peacefully. Many constitutional democracies, in addition, were themselves instituted by movements acting in the name of some variety of pluralist thinking. This problem has given rise to variations on the central argument that strong and persistent interests should not be suppressed. For example, Kingsley Widmer has widened and made more rigorous the conditions under which an interest can be said to have legitimately gained a hearing: "Open institutions must really presuppose that criticism will not only be accepted but understood, that protest will not only be allowed but responsively answered, that resistance to abuses will not only grow but modify the conditions."[16] Thus, he argues that democracy requires that protest be listened to seriously, rather than merely permitted. He contends that the activities of protest groups on the American left are understandable in terms of the notion that only the form, and not the substance, of democracy is present in the United States: "Many of the responses of current dissent appear impolite, intransigent, extreme and destructive in terms of how our institutions *should* respond rather than in terms of their real rejection or distortion of most criticism and change."[17]

Widmer's argument confronts the problem of justifying violence of the dispossessed in a constitutional democracy by redefining the democratic process. However, the argument still faces the traditional problems associated with the pluralist position. Widmer claims that democracies should understand criticism, answer it responsively, and act to modify the conditions criticized. While the first two conditions are recommendations about the democratic process itself, the third condition concerns the content of policy. Widmer merely assumes that the interests represented by the protesters somehow have a higher moral standing than those represented by established authorities. He certainly does not mean to say that every criticism presented by a protesting group should be acted upon favorably, for this would often place officials in the position of having to act on contradictory policies. Yet he does not show that the programs of the left are morally superior to other programs. Such demonstration appears to be impossible in the pluralist context. Thus, Widmer's justification of violence is at an ideological disadvantage to the justifications offered by legitimist and expansionist ideologists.

Violence to End Violence

The ideological disadvantage in pluralist modes could only be overcome by somehow universalizing the claims to self-determination expressed by dispossessed groups. This task was first carried out by the Marxists, whose arguments have constituted a model for justifying revolutionary violence in the twentieth century, whether undertaken by social classes, nationalities, or

other groups. The key to Marxist and related justifications of violence is the claim that violence committed by dispossessed groups is legitimate when it is aimed at putting an end to violence as a means of resolving human disputes and allocating resources and social functions. This universal aim can be used to veil more parochial aims, and puts the ideologist on an equal footing with opponents who draw upon natural law or cultural superiority arguments to justify violence.

One of the most serious recent attempts to justify revolutionary violence from a neo-Marxist perspective has been undertaken by Maurice Merleau-Ponty in *Humanism and Terror*. The core of Merleau-Ponty's argument is the claim that "all we know is different kinds of violence and we ought to prefer revolutionary violence because it has a future of humanism." [18] Thus, the "question is not to know whether one accepts or rejects violence, but whether the violence with which one is allied is 'progressive' and tends toward its own suspension or toward self-perpetuation." [19] Under this interpretation, each human being is faced with the choice of attempting to make a revolution aimed at ending violence, and accepting what it involves, or of seeking at every moment to treat each human being as an end in himself, and thereby accomplishing nothing but strenghening the forces of exploitation. Thus, Merleau-Ponty claims that both the anti-Communist and the fanatical Communist are in bad faith. The anti-Communist refuses to recognize that violence is universal, in that the exploitation of dispossessed classes and nationalities is as violent as the activities involved in political insurrection. The fanatical Communist refuses to see that violence is such a denial of humanity that "no one can look violence in the face." [20] Thus, Merleau-Ponty maintains that "the essential task of Marxism is to find a violence which recedes with the approach of man's future." [21]

Merleau-Ponty is led to this position through a keen analysis of the characteristics of pluralist consciousness. Thus, he shows how the Marxist justification grows out of the problems involved in negating natural law and expansionist absolutism. He argues that it is the contingency of the future which accounts for the violent acts of those in power. The course of history cannot be predicted with certainty, and this situation results in attempts by elites to gain control over the future by employing violent means to limit the freedom of the dispossessed and thereby protect their privileges. However, Merleau-Ponty observes that this very contingency of the future, which accounts for the violent acts of those in power, "by the same token deprives these acts of all legitimacy, or equally legitimates the violence of their opponents." [22] Under this condition it becomes impossible for any interest to demonstrate rationally that it has a superior claim to realize its projected future. The only way out of this bind is to move beyond the present and aim political action at a humanist future in which violence recedes. The central meaning of Merleau-Ponty's thought has been captured by a sympathetic reviewer: "Can we find a violence which is 'revolutionary and capable of creating human relations among men'? This is the problem which stands first on the agenda of our times."[23]

Merleau-Ponty's argument rests on several assumptions which are central to a Marxist justification of revolutionary violence. The first assumption is that violence can be marginalized through political action, including violent action. He has not proven his point by presenting an either/or choice between following the categorical imperative and making revolution. This choice is only plausible if the definition of violence is widened to include all acts in which human beings are not treated as ends in themselves. While it is Merleau-Ponty's privilege to widen the definition of violence this far, it does make it questionable whether revolutionary action will succeed in marginalizing violence. At most, Merleau-Ponty can claim that one should act to extend the range of situations in which human beings are treated as ends in themselves. The means of accomplishing this goal then remain a matter of empirical determination, and may work out never to involve the use of physical force. The second assumption, which Merleau-Ponty does not make explicitly, is that one can identify the group or groups which are most likely to act on the premise of marginalizing violence. The experience of many leftist regimes in the twentieth century does not hold out much hope that this identification can be made with ease. Underlying both of these assumptions is the fundamental Marxist principle that economic exploitation is at the root of other forms of violence, and that this exploitation can be ended through the action of a worker's movement. This principle has not yet been subjected to a test and remains an article of faith. It is perhaps for this reason that the Marxist justification of revolutionary violence is so ideologically compelling. The idea of a violence to marginalize or end violence, committed in the cause of a universal humanism, serves as a way out of the problem of moral relativism posed by pluralist approaches to violence. However, in giving the ideologist supporting dispossessed groups the same self-confidence and certainty as the legitimist and the expansionist, it deprives him of his empiricism. In its purest form, as expressed by such thinkers as Vivas, the pluralist mode has the advantage of not resorting to undemonstrable principles, such as the natural law of the legitimist, the "inherent superiority" of the expansionist, or the non-violent future of the Marxist. It appeals to perception of conflicts of interest and to immediate sympathy and identification. However, sympathy is notoriously unstable, and ideologists have found that Bentley's "is" and "must" are far more potent than the "maybe's" of such thinkers as Vivas. This is perhaps one reason why Marxism and related nationalist and socialist ideologies came to supplant utilitarianism as frameworks in which political violence is justified.

At least one recent writer has attempted to render the Marxist argument more empirical. Barrington Moore draws Merleau-Ponty's distinction between progressive and exploitative violence, but adds the idea that the progressive character of violence must be subject to empirical test: "(There is a) crucial moral and political distinction between the violence of the oppressors and of those who resist oppression. By itself, however, this important distinction remains rather abstract. We need to inquire whether the violence of the oppressed has made important contributions to human freedom in the past and whether it may continue to make such contributions today."[24] Moore argues that a case can be made that the violence of the left has traditionally functioned in the West to make the center more progressive. This is in contrast to the argument that leftist violence brings on rightist counterviolence. Either of these two arguments can be defended plausibly by supporting historical data, and neither of them can be assumed to be true *a priori*. Having argued that leftist violence actually has made contributions to human freedom, Moore goes on to state that revolutionary violence, defined as "the deliberate use of lower-case resentments and hatreds to bring about qualitative changes in the political and social order," works only when revolutionary rhetoric does not outrun "the real possibilities inherent in a given historical situation."[25] Thus, Moore is appealing for a more empirical Marxist justification of violence. In making this appeal he is steering Marxism back towards the purer forms of pluralist thinking based on moral relativism. It becomes an empirical judgment based on individual observation whether or not a particular set of violent actions is tending in the direction of increasing human freedom. In the light of the discussion of Marxism above, it is likely that such an empirical approach would reduce ideological effectiveness.

Pluralism and the Status Quo

In the opening sections of this chapter we have concentrated on the pluralist mentality, particularly insofar as it is employed to justify violence by those seeking to overthrow the established order. In contrast, the case study that follows serves to illustrate that this mode may be used to give legitimacy to the status quo, too. Moreover, we have deliberately chosen this particular case even though, at first, it would not appear to fall within the mode of rationalization discussed above. This helps us demonstrate the immense variety and flexibility of various modes of ideological rationalization as they are applied to specific political issues.

Those temperamentally suited to the pluralist ideology are not lightly moved to violence. Or to reverse this, cultural relativism, one of the hallmarks of pluralism, does not come easily to those committed enough to be moved to the risks and responsibilities of violent behavior. One senses that rather than subscribe to the somewhat bland maxim that no societal order is intrinsically superior, they would feel more comfortable, as advocates of violence, with the more visceral inducements of the legitimist and expansionist modes of violent thought. But the advocacy of structures of super- and subordination is out of favor. More universally defensible cognitive modes must be created, refined, and deployed. This and the other themes of pluralist thinking are woven together, albeit in a somewhat incongruous and tattered fabric, in the tragic juxtapositions that presently prevail in South Africa. In the following section we are chiefly concerned with thought patterns and rationalizations for societal forms and policies. Unfortunately, we cannot discuss at length the social consequences of these patterns, though we will touch upon them peripherally.

South Africa

This temporal, though by no means mercurial, quality of certain expressions of societal norms (one suspects that the norms themselves are more constant) as they relate to violence can be seen by tracing the evolution of South African Afrikaner thinking about race relations from *baasskap* through *apartheid* to the more euphemistic "separate development." Of course, the idea of racial domination in the Union and now the Republic of South Africa is not exclusively a creature of Afrikanerdom. English-speaking white settlers did their share to encourage, adapt to, and reinforce social patterns first set by the Dutch and French settlers to the Cape. But, theoretically at least, the refinement of various ideas and policies now collectively labelled as *apartheid* can be identified with and attributed to Afrikaner intellectuals and to Afrikaner politicians and spokesmen, especially since 1948 when the Nationalist Party came to power. [26] The evolution of political ideas associated with racial domination in South Africa provides a good case study of how political ideologies and practices may be manipulated to exploit the opportunities and demands of the times.

The so-called "native question" has perplexed various South African and British governments since before the turn of the century. In its earliest forms such derivative policies were essentially ad hoc responses to pressures from various white constituencies and interests, constituencies obsessed with economic exploitation, material privilege, communal identity, and survival. The term *baasskap* has been widely used to describe those policies, and the state of mind that engendered them. *Baasskap* was marked by unquestioning commitment to the maintenance of the master-servant relationship between South Africa's white and African populations, with the coloured and Indian peoples ranged between these two, but still subject to white mastery. In this hierarchical relationship of super- and sub-ordination there had been widespread acceptance among the white rulers of the doctrine of racial superiority that was, itself, felt to be a product of the innate biological superiority of all white men as individuals and of the white race as a collectivity. This conviction of superiority encouraged the various settler states that were spawned in South Africa to rely upon violence and warfare to maintain the "natural" order of things. Some sought Biblical sanction for their attitudes. *Die Boer met sy Bybel en sy Roer* (the Boer with his Bible and his rifle) became the symbolic expression of the Afrikaner's role in history. The Bible stood for Calvinist purity and the rifle for racial domination. Others tempered their station with a paternalistic concern for "their natives" for whom they were "trustees" or "guardians" in perpetuity. Still others were content to enjoy the material, psychological, and practical advantages such an order bestowed upon them, without bothering to erect an elaborate rationalization. If there was a philosophy of *baasskap* it was vaguely formulated and unsystematically but effectively implemented. *Baasskap* was, at heart, a way of life, not a philosophy or a set of laws.

The cultural residue of *baasskap* still prevails, as do its policy vestiges in what is frequently described by "enlightened" South Africans as "petty apartheid." It can be seen daily in the demeaning and ubiquitous racial indignities growing out of segregated and rarely equal public facilities, the countless phobic ways races are kept apart in private and economic intercourse, and in the exclusion altogether of men of color from many private and some public facilities for which there are no non-white counterparts. With the increasing political sophistication of all segments of the South African population it became difficult for *baasskap* alone to sustain the status quo. It served to exacerbate race relations without sufficiently serving as a barrier for racial intercourse and as a defense of white supremacy.

In the 1930s and the 1940s Afrikaner intellectuals felt the need to devise a more comprehensive theory, indeed a massive philosophy of race relations that would at once embody the domination and "preservation" of South African whites and, hopefully to them, the Afrikaner community. To some the issue was not so much what attitudes whites should hold toward the black people of South Africa, but rather what should be their own attitudes toward their own community, comprising not just the living people of their own cultural stock, but also their forefathers and their own successors, in the sense of a *volk*. To them *apartheid*, as their philosophy came to be called, was ostensibly an effort to conserve their embattled *volk* community. To others, those perhaps more conscious of the potential for race conflict in South Africa, the idea of greater physical separation of the races, at least in their residential locations, became the sensible approach not just to the maintenance of group cohesion, but to the continuation of white supremacy as well. The outside world was told increasingly about the need for racial separation. To the internal electorate, an almost exclusively white electorate in the 1940s, the cause of white supremacy was stressed. Reliance upon scriptural support diminished and increasingly secular, pragmatic bases for *apartheid* were advanced.

Apartheid became, in many ways, a transitional rather than the "final" response to the "race question" in South Africa. In a 1948 election manifesto the Nationalist Party capsulized its *apartheid* thinking in these terms:

> It is a policy which sets itself the task of preserving and safeguarding the racial identity of the white population of the country; of likewise preserving and safeguarding the identity of the indigenous peoples as separate racial groups, with opportunities to develop into self-governing national units; of fostering the inculcation of national consciousness, self-esteem and mutual regard among the various races of the country. . . .

> In general terms our policy envisages segregating the most important ethnic groups and sub-groups in their own areas where every group will be enabled to develop into a self-sufficient unit. We endorse the general principle of territorial segregation of the Bantu and the Whites. . . . The Bantu in the urban areas should be regarded as migratory citizens not entitled to political or social rights equal to those of the Whites. The process of detribalization should be arrested.[27]

Gradually, but systematically and comprehensively, the Nationalist government sought to separate the various racial groups in all facets of social interaction except the economic, and even in the economic some important facets of life were segregated, at least in horizontal *baasskap* terms. After 1948 an elaborate structure of laws was constructed piecemeal to bring about the *apartheid* state. Before then the segregation patterns were less systematic and more casually enforced. After 1948, "group areas" within designated white municipalities brought about the greatest dislocation as tens of thousands of non-whites were "relocated," i.e., forcefully removed from their residential neighborhoods to townships on the outskirts of cities. Through a policy known as "influx control" largely unsuccessful efforts were made to stem the flow of African migrants to cities that were supposed to be "white by night." These were migrant laborers in the sense that they lacked any permanency in "white areas" and family life largely disentegrated. The new concentrations of African workers thus became more manageable for purposes of suppressing potential organized dissent and insurgency. Separation was effected without the slightest pretense of self-determination. It was noted, however, by the obsessively defensive Afrikaner government that such policies were the necessary first steps in protecting the integrity of "Christian civilization" in South Africa of which Afrikanerdom is ostensibly the dominant segment. Even at some significant economic costs, this medium-range separation was consummated.

In af effort to have both racial separation and access to a large exploitable laboring class, a massive coercive police arm enforced *apartheid* policies. In this regard the *apartheid* state was founded upon and depended upon violence to maintain itself. The various laws passed to administer the growing *apartheid* edifice and to harass and eradicate groups and individuals seeking to overthrow or dismantle the regime no less than the regime's repressive enforcement policies testified to the government's determination to rely upon force or the fear of violent reprisal. The ostensible compliance with the liberal principle of the rule of law and the trappings of Western democratic procedures in intra-white politics, in international affairs, and even in some procedural aspects of *apartheid* law failed to mask the transparent central consideration that what really counted in South Africa was to keep the lid on real and potential non-white opposition. To this end, the regime was sedulously determined to use *any* means necessary to maintain white dominance. In uncompromising terms the late Prime Minister H. F. Verwoerd told his countrymen: "We want to make South Africa White . . . . Keeping it White can only mean one thing, namely White domination, not leadership, not guidance, but control, supremacy."[28] Domination, control, and supremacy are words that connote the legitimacy of violence in the achievement and defense of a preferred order, particularly in a society with the demographic characteristics of South Africa amid the geopolitical realities of southern Africa. It is a matter of categorical choice. In another context Dr. Verwoerd inflexibly put it: "Concession is surrender. White South Africans faced a simple choice between survival and downfall, and they would defend themselves in all ways, even with the rifle if it could not be otherwise."[29]

But *apartheid* had not been a static idology, as those charged with the responsibility of achieving separation quickly realized. Even as its dictates were being implemented, Afrikaner theoreticians were carrying it through to its logical conclusions. The outside world came to see *apartheid* as a thinly veiled and legalized refinement of *baasskap*. South African racial policies would need to be updated and streamlined for outside and even internal consumption. In addition, critics on the right within South Africa argued that *apartheid* did not go far enough. In their eyes there was still too much contact between the races. They were haunted by the fear that racial interaction, in any context, would lead ultimately to the extinction of their community.

The result of this continual battering from both the right and left internally and from the left (there are hardly any to the right) externally was a rethinking that rendered the more sophisticated ideology of "separate development." It was a grand design for a final solution to the "native question." To the outside world emphasis was to be laid on the aspects of self-determi-

nation and the ultimate independence of diverse African peoples. In the en-
visioned utopia, cultural differences were to be championed and racial distinctions deemphasized (except that a single white "nation" was to be
forged). At least this is what the *verligte* (broad-minded) wing of the Nationalist Party sought. Given the Afrikaner argument of the unbridgeable and acceptable "natural" cultural differences between the various communities that
inhabit South Africa and given that "group antagonisms seem to be inevitable when two peoples in contact with each other may be distinguished by
differentiating characteristics, either inborn or cultural, and are actual or potential competitors," the most sensible avenue for the prevention of conflict
and violence is to separate physically such groups on territorial terms.[30] We
can see here a version of the "violence to end violence" argument in the pluralist mode.

Thus a "grand *apartheid*" was to be constructed, a "vertical" geographical separation to replace and make unnecessary "horizontal" segregation
that is based upon a caste-like structure for the entire territory. In the words
of one early theorist of separate development: "The ideal solution to the race
question in South Africa will result from the territorial separation of the diverse racial groups, permitting each community to pursue its own socio-economic evolution and develop its own form of government."[31] However, the
so-called "self-determination" was in fact reserved, particularly in the early
phases of implementation, to the dominant minority white government. But
once the Nationalist government declared for a policy of separate development under H. F. Verwoerd and J. B. Vorster, it began the Herculean
task of establishing territorial entities known as Bantu Homelands for each
major subgroup of South and South West African blacks. Segments of the
white electorate, particularly the business interests, opposed separate development. It was also a direct challenge to the existing character of South Africa's economic development. A truly equitable distribution of the territory
was never seriously contemplated, though small elements of the white population advocated such a division of the assets of the country.[32] Nevertheless,
the vertical compartmentalization of South Africa's peoples continued as "re-
dundant" urbanized Africans were "endorsed out" of white areas and re-
turned, almost always against their wishes, to tribal "homelands" they never
really knew. [33]

Much of the detailed reality of separate development has still to be worked
out in the day-to-day political arena. As it presently stands, separate development in theory calls for the massive, and invariably forceful if need be, re-
location of various African peoples to their tribal homelands. Meanwhile,
new governments embodying some quasitraditional polity are to be established there that will, in concert with the white government in Pretoria, work
towards the "independence" of these Bantustans. The pace and nature of the

devolution of responsibility to "national," read tribal, leaders depends on numerous vague criteria, none of which have been defined by Pretoria. The ultimate decisions regarding a Bantustan's readiness for self-government and independence will *de facto* reside in the hands of the central government. In many ways this provides a relatively controllable safety-valve outlet for incipient African nationalism. It also serves as a smoke screen to confuse Western and African critics that may be inclined to vacillate on how to deal with racist South Africa. By emphasizing differences between various African peoples, and by separating them physically, greater control can be exerted by Pretoria in preventing a united non-white or even a united African front against white supremacy. Pretoria is the hub of any potential subsystem of partially or fully independent states. It alone would maintain contact with each of the outlying entities. Levers of communication and hence of power are still to be concentrated in minority white hands. Even if ultimately a confederation of the various components should be established, as some Nationalist officials have intimated, white South Africa would always be *primus inter pares*. And this pertains not merely to the structural configuration of power in South Africa—the economic pattern that would evolve would be even more one-sided and concentrated. For all this the more palatable term of "coexistence" is increasingly coming into vogue in government circles.

If Pretoria is successful in re-tribalizing South Africa's African, this would facilitate her "divide and rule" strategy. It would be naive to contend that the Africans in South Africa are a single people or nation, though some revolutionary African nationalists seek to foster this impression. But this is not an impossible dream on their part. In certain contexts, for example in the mining compounds and in certain townships, it is practically a reality. Indeed, given the present population patterns in South Africa it would be a strong likelihood in the course of the next few decades if not sooner. Separate development seeks as well to address itself to this potential challenge. Separate development, if successful, would prevent such a harmonization of African interests and aspirations. Instead of a single, modern, Westernized nationalist movement emerging there would more likely be an internally divided, increasingly racially defined ethnocentrism. [34] As Pretoria would have it, several varieties of the "noble savage" would emerge, unspoiled by Western culture and unexploited by Western economic encroachments. In fact, however, it would be but a parody on traditional tribal structure, as Pretoria-approved if not appointed puppets administer destitute territories on behalf of the status quo. Given most politicians' (including South Africa's black puppets') political instincts to opt for survival even within a fundamentally unacceptable system, many may perceive themselves as creatures of two constituencies, the white government and their own people. As such, they may seek to maximize their options and rewards within the system. We may see such Bantustan leaders pay lip service to the principles of separate development at the same time that they persistently and pragmatically are testing the limits of autonomy, continually pressing for greater authority and responsibility and for a greater share of the resources of the country. This has already begun, and with far greater persistence and vehemence than many had originally imagined. By such strategies and tactics, it is conceivable that the central government may yet be forced to give a specific content to separate development that Pretoria may not have originally intended, or they may be compelled to make good on vague promises lightly advanced years earlier.

Both racial parties are maneuvering to survive in what they see as a hostile environment. Both are experimenting in their efforts to give positive content to vaguely and incompletely defined ideological principles that had been heretofore defined by only one dominant element in a complex society. The bargaining process may not be as formalistically structured as political scientists may desire, but it goes on nevertheless.

Pluralism and Apartheid

One might ask at this point: Where does the pluralist position enter into this discussion? It seems most apparent when we examine the normative and cognitive threads running throughout the evolving *apartheid* fabric.

The ideologies of *apartheid* and separate development are founded upon a fundamentally anti-liberal doctrine. Classical European liberalism rests upon the presumption that the individual has certain rights and duties that deserve to be defended and maintained. He exists independent of society and society is obliged to secure for the individual his inalienable rights. In practical terms, a good deal of daily political struggle in professedly liberal systems entails the continual task of defining and redefining the limits of individual liberties insofar as they impinge upon those of the community and those of the community as they relate to the individual. But *apartheid,* as a theoretical construct, concentrates on the collectivity. The individual is regarded chiefly as an integral, organic component of a larger being. This is the essence of Afrikaner solidarity. Man has no existence outside of the community. His creative potentialities can never be realized if he divorces himself from his communal body. Self-realization can be obtained only in a community with which he identifies. If he is separated from that community he becomes alienated. "Apartheid is opposed," writes A. James Gregor, "to the abstract humanitarianism of liberal individualism." [35] In reality, of course, many Afrikaners who still identify with the *volk* are capable of seeing its fallacies and weaknesses. Other Afrikaners have broken with the rigid constrictions of group thought and have, in effect, been ostracized by the *volk.* Still, Afrikanerdom is not all that united. There is a good deal of intense intellectual ferment about racial issues. Nevertheless, the pretense of unity and group solidarity is, in theory, presented to *uitlanders*, those outside of the *laager*. [36] In theory, at least, man develops, matures, succeeds only as a part of a larger collectivity. Apart from his community he loses all *raison d'etre*, he becomes flaccid, content-less, nothing. This empirical model is then given normative content and hence is tailor-made to reinforce the solidarity of Afrikanerdom and to justify and lend moral muscle to the social strictures and policies of *apartheid*. Coupled with Biblical sanction, this presents the *volk* with a God-given right to exist and to defend itself against all assaults by other communities, by individuals, and by other philosophies. It becomes, in a way, a natural law justification for violence at the same time that it appeals to the reality of cultural diversity, a modern justification for violence. The *apartheid* doctrine is, itself, an obvious creature of the crises evolution of Afrikanerdom, with its violent history and its Calvinist roots.

Hence, there are repeated, unambiguous declarations of the so-called *laager* mentality with reference to a fight to the death to prevent integration, liberalism and, supposedly, the extinction of Afrikanerdom. A few examples will suffice. In the initiation ceremony of the *Ruiterwag*, a now dissolved junior wing of the *Broederbond* (a secret power elite which many had regarded as the cabal-like core of Afrikanerdom), the initiant was told:

> The struggle that our fathers began,
> Will rage till we have died or won.
> That is the oath of Young South Africa. [37]

The Minister of Defense phrased it in these picturesque terms: "We will fight till the blood rises to the horses' bit—but I can tell them [the African leaders] that the blood won't be on the bits of our horses only." [38] *Die Transvaler* of Johannesburg pugnaciously spoke for the *volk:* "When fighting is necessary we will not hesitate. A time comes in a people's history when not only reason must speak, but also its blood. That time has now dawned." [39]

Although more sophisticated Afrikaners may tell questioning foreigners that no culture is intrinsically superior, or at least that biological race differences are not indices of innate superiority or inferiority, it does not follow that no particular order is better for them and for those whose lives touch upon them closely. Therefore, they would argue that it is legitimate, indeed just and necessary, for them to use violent means to establish and then maintain their regime, just as it is illegitimate to impose an alien normative order on peoples of a radically different culture. We are expected to believe that all the South African government really wants for the African is that he develop, mature, and appreciate the reality of his own "self-determination" when in fact it is an imposed "other-determination." It is this sort of reasoning that seeks to rationalize (as well as to minimize the need for) direct physical violence in the service of self-determination for the dominant group. After all, in the pluralist mode of thought, force is normal and to be expected in inter-group relations.

Separate development as a de-ideologized ideology is, contrary to widely held opinion, not an outdated, passé philosophy. [40] What it seeks to accomplish may be obsolete and antediluvian. But how it is advanced and packaged seems calculated to appeal to peoples who live in states with minority group problems of acculturation, assimilation, and integration. Separate development can be seen as a modernized version of colonialism, in which the colonized people live within the state's boundaries rather than outside them. [41] It has been well labelled "domestic neo-colonialism."[42] It may be a distillation of previous South African experiences and their interpretation of European experiences with colonialism and decolonization, employing more sophisticated but no less transparent devices such as indirect rule, educational socialization, family controls, border industries, "book of life" identity systems, and many others. Whatever the appearances, no system would wittingly be instituted by a white-dominated regime that endangers its continued advantageous control of the entire South African subcontinent.

We must point out, however, that such reasoning could, with some adaptations, be employed by the subordinate groups seeking liberation from the imposed order. Having gained sufficient power to alter the status quo, a ready-made ideological rationalization for the employment of power exists. It was used by the Boers against the British at the turn of the century. It could be used by South Africa's Africans in the future. By calling for "Black Power" as have some younger leaders, an embryonic African political element poses a difficult dilemma for the regime.[43] It is, after all, an "acceptable" appeal that the white government cannot regard as entirely unfair, even though it may wish to crush its proponents. It must be remembered that it was Dr. Verwoerd, the chief architect of separate development, who once said: "Many derogatory things were said about black nationalism in particular, but world history showed that the desire of a group or a nation to become free could not be frustrated for ever."[44] It is an appeal to group norms similar to that on which Afrikaner consciousness and solidarity is based. In theory separate development urges group awareness among the various peoples in their "homelands." They are entreated to strive for group dignity and self-reliance. The problem is that the "Black Power" appeal seeks to transcend primordial loyalties and to see the oneness of African existence in white South Africa. Thus in the eyes of the Pretoria regime "Black Power" is separate development writ too large, since "natural," static, primordial communities are to take precedence over "artificial," acculturated, i.e., Westernized, communities which, presumably by definition, are not legitimate communities at all. Here lies the crux of the issue itself: What is the nature of culture contact and exchange, and can cultures be frozen or even, like

Humpty Dumpty, be pieced together again in a form acceptable to a dominant minority and a potentially powerful numerical majority?

We may have some difficulty in seeing separate development as being basically a product of pluralist thinking. This is understandable for essentially two reasons. First, the effects of these policies would not appear to demonstrate any awareness of cultural or moral relativism. The net effects of separate development, despite what the South African government tells us, are so one-sidedly advantageous to the whites that we find it hard to believe that it is not an outgrowth of either a legitimist or an expansionist mode of analysis. In part, of course, it is. Second, we are faced with the problem of apparent discrepancies between professed government policy, actual policy, and the known racial attitudes of the bulk of the white population in South Africa. A pluralist mode of reasoning, it would appear, is chiefly expressed in the official rationale for the sacrifices, impositions, and the attendant violence that has accompanied the establishment and enforcement of policies of *apartheid* and separate development. As such it represents a modernized and hence more serviceable ideology for South Africa's repressive racial relations.

NOTES

1. Kingsley Widmer, "The Rage Against Violence," *Nation,* 20 July 1970, p. 46.

2. Ibid., p. 48.

3. Ibid., p. 48.

4. Martin J. Hillenbrand, *Power and Morals* (New York: Columbia University Press, 1949), p. 132.

5. Robert J. McNamara, "The Ethics of Violent Dissent," *Proceedings of the Academy of Political Science* 29 (1968): p. 143.

6. Ernest W. Ranly, "The Ways of Violence," *America,* 12 September 1970, p. 143.

7. Peter J. Riga, "Paul VI and Violence," *The Catholic World* 200: 253.

8. World Council of Churches, "Violence: A Christian Reassessment," *Current* (May 1968): 120.

9. Ibid., p. 121.

10. Frederick D. Webber, "Riots and Respect for Law," *The Catholic World* 200: 70.

11. Eliseo Vivas, "Force in Empirical Ethics," *Ethics* 49 (October 1938): 85.

12. Ibid., p. 85.

13. Ibid., p. 89.

14. Ibid., p. 91.

15. Ibid., p. 92.

16. Kingsley Widmer, "Why Dissent Turns Violent," *Nation,* 7 April 1969, p. 425.

17. Ibid., p. 428.

18. Maurice Merleau-Ponty, *Humanism and Terror* (Boston: Beacon Press, 1969), p. 107.

19. Ibid., p. 1.

20. Ibid., p. 2.

21. Ibid., p. xviii.

22. Ibid., p. xxxvi.

23. Dick Howard, "Review of *Humanism and Terror*," *Commonweal*, 27 November 1970, p. 226.

24. Barrington Moore, Jr., "Thoughts on Violence and Democracy," *Proceedings of the Academy of Political Science* 29 (1968): p. 3

25. Ibid., p. 6.

26. The definitive history of the idea as interpreted by Afrikaner intellectuals is: N.J. Rhoodie and H.J. Venter, *Apartheid: A Socio-Historical Exposition of the Origin and Development of the Apartheid Idea* (Amsterdam: De Bussy, 1960).

27. As quoted in: Colin and Margaret Legum, *South Africa: Crisis for the West* (New York: Praeger, 1964), pp. 49-50.

28. January 25, 1963, as quoted in: Pierre L. van den Berghe, *South Africa: A Study of Conflict* (Berkeley and Los Angeles: University of California Press, 1967), p. 118.

29. *The Star* (Johannesburg), 21 September 1963.

30. *Rejoinder filed by the Government of the Republic of South Africa.* South West Africa Cases (*Ethiopia and Liberia* v. *The Republic of South Africa*). International Court of Justice (1964), I, 446. As quoted in A. James Gregor, *Contemporary Radical Ideologies: Totalitarian Thought in the Twentieth Century* (New York: Random House, 1968), p. 249.

31. G. Cronje, *Regverdige Raase-Apartheid* (Johannesburg: CXV, 1947), p. 155; as quoted in Gregor, *Contemporary Radical Ideologies,* p. 251.

32. Some proposals on territorial redistribution are embodied in Leo Marquard, *A Federation of Southern Africa* (London: Oxford University Press, 1971); and the results of the symposium at Natal University entitled, "Partition—an English-speaking point of view." This was reported in the *Sunday Times* (Johannesburg), 28 August 1966; *Rand Daily Mail* (Johannesburg), 27 August 1966; and the *Natal Mercury* (Durban), 29 August 1966. See also the comments on partition in *South Africa's Political Alternatives: Report of the Political Commission of the Study Project on Christianity in Apartheid Society.* SPRO-CAS Publication Number 10 (Johannesburg, SPRO-CAS, 1973), pp. 106-26, especially pp. 113-17.

33. Cosmas Desmond, O.F.M., *The Discarded People: An Account of African Resettlement in South Africa* (Harmondsworth: Penguin, 1971).

34. See Heribert Adam, *Modernizing Racial Domination: The Dynamics of South African Politics* (Berkeley and Los Angeles: University of California Press, 1971), p. 40.

35. Gregor, *Contemporary Radical Ideologies,* p. 237.

36. During the Afrikaner settlers' trek north and east from the Cape in the nineteenth century, in the evenings they would arrange their wagons into a defensive enclosure to enable them to fight off raids from Bantu war parties. This wagon arrangement was called a *laager.* In modern parlance, *laager* is often used as a synonym for the Afrikaner *volk* or community, and particularly of its most parochial, inner-oriented facets.

37. The entire ceremony, as reported in the *Rand Daily Mail* (Johannesburg), 3 July 1958, is reprinted in: William Henry Vatcher, Jr., *White Laager: The Rise of Afrikaner Nationalism* (New York: Praeger, 1965), pp. 285-87.

38. Mr. J.J. Fouché in *The Star*, 6 April 1963.

39. *Die Transvaler* (Johannesburg), 1 June 1963.

40. Adam, *Modernizing Racial Domination.*

41. Leo Marquard, *South Africa's Colonial Policy: Presidential Address, 1957* (Johannes-

burg: South African Institute of Race Relations, 1957): and Gwendolen M. Carter, Thomas Karis, and N.M. Stultz, *South Africa's Transkei: The Politics of Domestic Colonialism* (Evanston, Illinois: Northwestern University Press, 1967).

42. Adam, *Modernizing Racial Domination,* p. 68.

43. Patrick Laurence, "Increase of Black Consciousness in South Africa," *The Star* (Weekly Air Edition), 19 February 1972, p. 11.

44. *Die Burger* (Cape Town), 9 October 1961; as quoted in Legum and Legum, *South Africa,* p. 55.

Chapter Five

Intrinsic Justifications of Violence

Until the twentieth century the vast majority of ideological apologists for violence have justified the use of violence as an efficient, or the most efficient, means to certain supposedly moral ends. Despite their many and serious differences, they have remained more or less consistent with Lasswell's principle that violence is an instrument of influence which is rationally applied only after a clear appraisal has been made of its use as a detail in the total context of political action. Thus, legitimist ideologists have defended violence as a means to maintaining a supposedly legitimate and already existing normative order against attack. Ultimately, legitimists argue that the force of the constituted authorities is justified as a way of neutralizing the violence of rebellious elements. Even in the more extreme versions of the expansionist's ideology, violence is a means rather than an end in itself. While Treitschke sometimes argued that superior might was an indicator of cultural excellence, he repeatedly maintained that whenever a "moral" end (for him, the triumph of a "superior" normative order) could be reached without violence, the non-violent course should be pursued. The catch, of course, was that Treitschke believed that in practice the triumph of German culture could only be assured through the application of violence. Finally, those who employ the pluralist justification regard violence either as a means to attaining self-determination for a group or as a way of putting an end to future violence altogether. For example, Merleau-Ponty argued that one has the option of either cooperating actively or passively in the violence of oppressors or implicating oneself in the violence of the oppressed.

In the twentieth century, a new dimension has been added to the justification of violence. For the ideologists that subscribe to what we call an intrinsic justification for violence, violence is either praised, or at least condoned, or rejected in principle as an integral part of a life-style. The shift from interpreting violence as an instrument of social engineering to viewing it as an element in a life-style has been accompanied by a strong concern with political psychology, and the ways in which collective violence directed at a normative order aids or hinders self-development. Thus, the focus on violence as an aspect of life-styles is closely linked to the recognition that committing or suffering acts of political violence can have profound effects on the course and meaning of personal life.

The concern with role of violence in self-development is perhaps a consequence of the violence unleashed in the modern era by groups attempting to impose normative orders upon other peoples and groups attempting to win self-determination, or the liberation of the "oppressed." Within the context of these struggles, human beings have been called upon to align themselves with one or another group, whose leaders were dedicated to using violence as an instrument for gaining power. Frequently, the appeals to engage in struggle posed severe conflicts between loyalties for the individual. Should the worker fight for his class or his nation? As many individuals became unclear about the normative order with which they were identified, it became possible for some ideologists to argue that violence itself might be beneficial for the individual in some circumstances. By committing acts of violence a person might be brought to identify himself strongly with a certain cause. Thus, while most of the ideologies of violence described in the preceding chapters assumed adherence to a cause prior to the commission of violent acts, intrinsic ideologies of violence recognize that the commission of violent acts may precede commitment to a cause, or at least identify and fortify such commitment. A person is brought into a violent social movement by persuading him about the alleged benefits that violence will bring to his personality and life-style.

Pervasive Violence

The most rudimentary intrinsic justifications of violence depend upon the claim that twentieth-century life is permeated by violence. Within these justifications, violence is defined broadly as any violation of human autonomy. Thus, the violent life-style is viewed as inseparably linked to the more general social climate of violence. Norman Mailer has discussed violence in this way. He distinguishes between social violence and personal violence. Social violence includes concentration camps and nuclear warfare, but "if one wants to carry the notion far enough, there are subtler forms of social violence such as censorship, or excessively organized piety, or charity drives."[1] Personal violence is "an act of violence by man or woman against other men or women," and is created by social violence as its antithesis.[2] For Mailer, personal violence is a reaction to the hollowness and artificiality of twentieth-century life. Violence is directly proportional to the power of the current social environment to deaden individuals' moods. Social violence is ubiquitous and larger than the ability of normal human beings to dominate. Thus, it is an "existential experience," which is "sufficiently unusual so that you don't know how it is going to turn out."[3] Saints are able to transcend this "instantaneous world of revelations," but psychopaths are broken by it or made murderous. In the present world, where social pestilence is everywhere, human beings in general become psychopaths in this sense. "The powerful impulse of the twentieth century" has been to defeat the impulse to personal violence "by elaborate social institutions which destroy the possibility of personal violence before it can have a free expression."[4] This construction of artificial institutions has "created an awareness of violence as electric as paranoia," and has made personal violence a way of breaking through to reality. Mailer concludes that "plastic" is the perfect metaphor for the nature of much contemporary violence, because plastic is artificial and often cracks unpredictably. Thus, personal violence cracks the social violence of a plastic society, and provokes a direct connection between human beings.

Colin Wilson has presented a similar argument. He claims that in a "highly organized and fairly affluent society, a kind of mental strain based on boredom and unfulfillment is bound to result" in violent acts by those people who are "strong-minded enough not to want to be 'organization men,' but incapable of seeing beyond an act of protest."[5] By fostering passivity when human fulfillment demands creative activity, the present society breeds sadistic violence, "because sadism is a disease of 'monstrous freedom.'"[6]

Wilson and Mailer are attempting to explain and perhaps condone or even justify sporadic and individual acts of violence undertaken in what they regard as a general climate of pervasive social violence. They qualify as ideologists of political violence because the acts that they describe are interpreted as symbolic attacks on a decadent social order, characterized by hypocrisy, artificiality, and the denial of humanity. Like other ideologists, Wilson and Mailer use "is" and "must" without hesitation. Mailer confidently asserts that personal violence "is" created by social violence, while Wilson claims that violence acts of protest are "bound" to result from a society which is boring and unsatisfying. Yet neither of these commentators is willing to assign a fully positive and creative function to violence as a part of a life-style. Their arguments may provide excuses for individuals who burst out in rage when they feel that they have been pushed beyond their limits. However, Mailer contrasts the saint, who transcends social violence, to the psychopath who is made murderous or is broken by it; and Wilson contrasts the strong minded person, who sees beyond acts of protest to positive alternatives, to the passive person, who can imagine no more than violent protest.

Perhaps the reason Wilson and Mailer hold back from fully approving of personal violence is that if personal violence were universalized its benefits would disappear. As long as violence as part of a life-style means violence towards anyone, it refutes itself. If the enemy is a depersonalized society, all are equally affected by it and anyone may be pushed to his limit at any time. There is no more reason to strike out against one person than another. Thus, for violence as part of a life-style to be used as a successful ideological justification of violence, there must be a separation made between enemies, upon whom it is legitimate to use violence, and friends, towards whom a posture of non-violence is maintained.

Violence and Solidarity

Intrinsic justifications of violence were offered at least as far back as the nineteenth century. The French conservative Joseph de Maistre wrote: "when the human spirit has lost its resilience through indolence, incredulity, and the gangrenous vices that follow an excess of civilization, it can be retempered only in blood."[7] Yet while de Maistre argued that "the arts, sciences, great enterprises, noble ideas, manly virtues," spring from war, he was not a fully successful ideologist, because he was ultimately led to admit that in war *"The innocent suffer for the benefit of the guilty."*[8] An appreciation of the ideological possibilities of viewing violence as part of a life-style awaited the work of Georges Sorel.

Sorel's justification of violence is contained in his work, *Reflections on Violence*. Like Wilson and Mailer he bases his argument on the ubiquity of violence in contemporary life. However, he traces social violence to the middle classes and contrasts it to proletarian violence which has creative functions. In Sorel's terminology, the primary distinction is between force and violence. The "object of force is to impose a certain social order in which the minority governs, while violence tends to the destruction of that order."[9] Sorel defines force very broadly and identifies it with capitalism: "whether force manifests itself under the aspect of historical acts of coercion, or of fiscal oppression, or of conquest, or labour legislation, or whether it is wholly bound up with the economic system, it is always a middle-class force labouring with more or less skill to bring about the capitalist order of society."[10] Violence is a proletarian reaction against middle-class force, and "should be employed only for acts of revolt."

The key to Sorel's justification of proletarian violence is that it is qualitatively different from middle-class force. This qualitative difference is present in Mailer's distinction between social and personal forms of violence, but Sorel collectivizes it. For Sorel, middle-class violence is integrally related to a life of stagnation, artificiality and hypocrisy, while proletarian violence is linked to a noble and heroic existence. This kind of qualitative distinction does not appear in legitimist, expansionist, or pluralist rationalizations, where violence is a means which has the same experiential quality whoever uses it. The crux of Sorel's case is that one can emancipate and improve oneself if he uses violence in concert with others against an oppressive enemy. While Mailer and Wilson were simply psychologists, Sorel is a social psychologist.

Sorel offers three specific justifications for proletarian violence. First, it unmasks the hypocrisy of middle-class domination by showing that capitalist social relations are based on brute force. By provoking counter-attacks from the enemy, proletarian violence shows the system for what it is and makes social relations more honest: "War, carried on in broad daylight, without hypocritical attenuation, for the purpose of ruining an irreconcilable enemy, excludes all the abominations which dishonoured the middle-class revolution of the eighteenth century. The apology for violence in this case is particularly easy."[11] Here proletarian violence works both pragmatically and as part of a life-style. Through unmasking hypocrisy, it both gains supporters for the worker's movement and furthers a life of honesty.

The second justification of violence offered by Sorel is that it increases the resolve, solidarity and confidence of revolutionaries. He states, in this connection, that he is "not at all concerned to justify the *perpetrators of violence*, but to inquire into the function of *violence of the working classes* in contemporary socialism."[12] Perhaps the central function that Sorel identifies for proletarian violence is its tendency to mark off class divisions sharply and stimulate revolutionary fervor. Violence continually rejuvenates the myth of the general strike, which gives direction and hope to the lives of workers. Struggling towards the day in which the capitalist state will fall from the impact of a great and uncompromising strike, workers find meaning in their lives. Proletarian acts of violence "are purely and simply acts of war; they have the value of military demonstrations, and serve to mark the separation of classes."[13]

Sorel's third justification of violence carries the argument that violence rejuvenates one step further. Here, the claim is that proletarian violence is inseparably linked to heroic morality. Sorel argues that proletarian violence is essentially disinterested because it "confines employers to their role of producers, and tends to restore the separation of classes, just when they seemed on the point of intermingling in the democratic marsh."[14] He hopes that the proletariat will force the middle classes to recover some of their former energy and revivify civilization. Thus, "proletarian violence, carried on as a pure and simple manifestation of the sentiments of class war, appears . . . as a very fine and a very heroic thing; it is at the service of the immemorial interests of civilisation; it is not perhaps the most appropriate method of obtaining immediate advantages, but it may save the world from barbarism."[15] Within this complex historical process the workers gain from proletarian violence because they are ennobled. Democracy, under capitalism, finds its strength in fostering sentiments of jealousy and vengeance throughout the population. These feelings cannot be supressed by sermons, but "social war, by making an appeal to the honour which develops so naturally in all organised armies" can eliminate them. Sorel concludes that "if this were the only reason we had for attributing a high civilising value to revolutionary syndicalism, this reason alone would, it seems to me, be decisive in favour of the apologists for violence."[16]

While Sorel is a more successful ideologist than either Mailer or Wilson, his apology for violence has an important structural weakness. He is addressing men "who are not hypnotised by the event of the day, but who think of the conditions of to-morrow."[17] Such people will be able to grasp the moral necessity of proletarian violence, despite the fact that it is not the most appropriate method of obtaining immediate advantages. They will see that the struggle is more important than the result, while the mass of workers will be heroes in spite of themselves. Thus, Sorel does not succeed in making postmodern justifications of violence into a popular ideology. The masses are motivated by the myth of the general strike, not by the ennobling characteristics of violence. A successful intrinsic ideology requires that violence be made a manifest object of political activity.

Therapeutic Violence

Through the use of a psychiatric approach, Frantz Fanon constructed a popular ideology for selective violence based upon an intrinsic justification for violent acts. To be sure, Fanon's contribution to political ideology extends to many facets of colonialism, neo-colonialism, and de-colonization. Our focus is on his approach to violence and tends to emphasize what is especially distinctive in his thought, although it may distort his total ideological contribution and constitution.

Concerned primarily with liberation from colonialism, Fanon, like other intrinsic thinkers, based his argument on the pervasive character of social violence. He begins his discussion by noting that through violent conquest European settlers created "natives" where there had only been human beings before: "Their first encounter was marked by violence and their existence together—that is to say the exploitation of the native by the settler—was carried on by dint of a great array of bayonets and cannons."[18] While in Europe, the working class is neutralized by the educational system, the churches, and "the structure of moral reflexes handed down from father to son," in the colonies "the agents of government speak the language of pure force" and the natives are advised "by means of rifle butts and napalm not to budge."[19] The settler brings "violence into the home and into the mind of the native."

The pervasive violence of the colonizer is supported by the rationalization that natives are sub-human and incapable of understanding reason. The colonial world is a "manichean world," in which the natives are pictured as absolute evil: "the native is declared insensible to ethics; he represents not only the absence of values, but also the negation of values."[20] This system of oppression is a "mass relationship," in which the "settler pits brute force against the weight of numbers."[21] Its most striking characteristic is that it creates profound aggressive drives throughout the native population.

At first the native turns "this aggressiveness which has been deposited in his bones against his own people." "Trapped in the tight links of the chains of colonialism," the native finds an outlet for aggression in tribal warfare, sectarian feuds, personal quarrels, and in such non-violent physical activities as dancing and tribal ritual. "Collective autodestruction" serves to distract the native from the crushing domination of the settler, but in the long run it is incapable of satisfying the native's persistent dream of replacing the settler. Thus, according to Fanon, there is no question of whether or not the native will resort to violence. Settler violence has made native violence inevitable. The crucial question is whether native violence will turn in a void or be directed towards liberation. During the struggle against colonialism the problem is "to lay hold of this violence which is changing direction," and turn it against the oppressor. As this redirection proceeds it becomes clear to the native that "this narrow world, strewn with prohibitions, can only be called in question by absolute violence."[22] The aim becomes putting the settler "out of the picture" once and for all. With the unfolding of the struggle, the native turns the Manichean world created by the settler against him. "Since (the natives) have decided to reply by violence, they therefore are ready to take all its consequences. They only insist in return that no reckoning should be kept either, for the others. To the saying 'all natives are the same' the colonized person replies, 'all settlers are the same.' "[23]

Fannon offers three specific justifications for native violence. First, like Sorel, he argues that violence invests the revolutionary character with "positive and creative qualities," since "each individual forms a violent link in the great chain, a part of the great organism of violence which has surged upward in reaction to the settler's violence in the beginning."[24] The emerging nation is bound together by a "cement which has been mixed with blood and anger." Violence is a great unifier of national sentiment, which allows the natives to overcome their petty jealousies and internecine strife.

However, Fanon goes beyond Sorel in his assignment of positive functions to violence. In addition to stimulating solidarity, violence leads to individual responsibility. Striking out violently against the settler symbolizes an irrevocable commitment to the liberation movement. Taking responsibility for violence by committing it "allows both strayed and outlawed members of the group to come back again and to find their place once more, to become integrated."[25] Thus, the native finds responsible freedom "in and through violence."

The idea that violence is tied to freedom leads to Fanon's final and most original justification of violence as part of life-style. Given his assumption that the settler has deposited aggressiveness in the native, the anti-colonial struggle becomes, for Fanon, more than merely a struggle for power. It becomes a way in which the native sheds the self-image imposed upon him by the settler and becomes a human being once again. Thus, violent decolonization, which is, we might add, in Fanon's view, the only real decolonization, is "the veritable creation of new men," in which "the 'thing' which had been colonized becomes man during the same process by which it frees itself."[26] It is in this process of self-development and transformation that violence serves its most profound function of decolonizing the mind: "at the level of individuals, violence is a cleansing force. It frees the native from his inferiority complex and from his despair and inaction; it makes him fearless and restores his self-respect."[27] Fanon claims that when a people has taken a violent part in its own liberation, it will not suffer demogogues because it will be composed of free human beings.

Through his argument that political violence is productive of mental health, Fanon makes violence a manifest object of political activity, thereby solving the problem in Sorel's thought. To be sure, there is an easy and not always justifiable transition between individual and group mental health. But the individual-aggregate distinction need not trouble us here. He also solved another problem present in post-modern ideologies of violence. While Wilson, Mailer, and Sorel, for example, all argued that there were qualitative differences between types of violence, none of them could make an iron-clad case for this claim. Particularly for Sorel, there is no obvious reason why a militant and expansive nationalism might not perform the same function of rejuvenation as a proletarian movement. Any uncompromising collective violence could be justified with Sorel's thought. This is not the case for Fanon, because only those oppressed by a manichean system gain purification and liberation through violence. Oppressors who use violence simply dehumanize themselves further because their problem is a superiority complex, not an inferiority complex. Thus, Fanon is enabled to make the distinction between violence of friend and violence of foe, which is essential to any successful ideology of violence. This resolution, however, has a price.

In order to make his argument, Fanon must make the blanket claim that settler violence is so pervasive that it has infected the personality of each native with the same disorder. There can be no escape from the social psychological determinism of colonialism and, therefore, no freedom for the native in his interpersonal relations. Further, Fanon must argue that violence, overtly or vicariously committed, is the only cure for the inferiority complex imposed by the settler. This claim that violence is the prescribed therapy for certain mental disorders runs up against the equally dogmatic assertion by advocates of non-violent life-styles (and sometimes advocates of legitimist ideologies) that violence tends to make one the same as one's enemy. Neither one of these absolute claims seems to have any scientific standing, and they confront each other starkly in contemporary political debate. Finally, Fanon's justification of violence depends upon the easy identification of an enemy. This makes his ideology particularly appropriate to anti-colonial revolution, but quite difficult to apply in other contexts. Perhaps one reason why Wilson and Mailer were so ambivalent and unsure about the positive functions of violence as part of a life-style is that there is no easily identifiable enemy in contemporary Western life. Without a clear enemy upon whom to vent anger, intrinsic justifications of violence tend to dissolve into half-hearted excuses for random outbursts. The world must be convincingly manichean for intrinsic ideologies to work, or else it must be basically uniform in the sense that there is a spark of good in every human being.

Like the other ideologies of violence, intrinsic justifications have an inherent instability, springing from the need of the ideologist to distinguish violence of friend from violence of foe. When violence as part of a life-style is condoned as an aspect of individualized rebellion, justifications tend to be half-hearted because the activity in question has no social direction. When such violence is justified as a component of a heroic life-style, the ideologial purist is driven to support any movement that maintains an atmosphere of struggle. Finally, even if there is a successful distinction between types of violence, the resulting ideology tends to have a narrowly restricted application to political situations and to be highly dogmatic.

There are few, if any, viable *movements* that embrace intrinsic ideologies of violence, as described in the preceding section. By and large, and hopefully forever, such a commitment to violence *qua* violence is confined to the realms of philosophical discourse and psychological abnormality rather than practice. Occasionally it may be associated with a few isolated individuals or occult-like groups with narrow followings. Isolated individuals and groups may subscribe to an intrinsic ideology of violence, but few groups will adopt it as their operative ideology. It is generally believed that such personalities that may be attracted to this sort of comradeship are mentally disturbed.

Violence, for some strange reason, holds a morbid fascination for many intellectuals, especially since it has become a legitimate field of study for social science. Some scholars and ideologists will explain violent group behavior in terms of an intrinsic rationalization of violence. But it is a long step from the realization that violence is an integral part of a society's life style to the glorification of violence or violent behavior. It is not the same to argue that "purposive" group violence yields commitment to the cause, and violence is itself a cause worthy of man's commitment. How would you go about winning converts to ritualized blood sacrifice, particularly for its unproven inherent benefits, and more particularly when such dicta run counter to the mores of every major social system the world has seen? Even in societies where the ritualization of violence has existed, it was invariably instrumental to other ends, and it was usually carried out by a small carefully defined segment of the population on a narrow segment of the population. It is conceivable, however, that should this planet become dangerously overpopulated such ideologies might emerge in more respectable form as a social psychological response to problems of density and impersonality. But shedding blood and destruction in and of themselves prove nothing. Few would be persuaded that the injustices of an old order can be washed away in a baptism of blood. Much less are their own personal fears and weaknesses susceptible to therapeutic violence. It is even less likely that a new and pure society can be born in a struggle based entirely on the mystical virtues of violence.

Should such movements, however, get off the ground, one can imagine that a very few followers may be won over, even though they may themselves only see violence as a *means* to the achievement of certain personal, socio-economic or political ends they value. We may also find snippets of intrinsic ideologies of violence displayed as corollaries, or as rhetorical baggage, attached to other sorts of ideologies of violence. But these are usually just complementary to such ideologies, not central to them. It may be helpful to look at a few historical as well as contemporary examples, since it is sometimes claimed that some of the movements to be mentioned have glorified violence as an end in itself.

Amongst nineteenth century Russian revolutionaries, for example, especially the anarchists and nihilists, there was a tendency to sing the praises of violence. In his first revolutionary essay, Michael Bakunin wrote that "the urge to destruction is at the same time a creative urge."[28] It was this sort of utterance that contributed to Bakunin's sensational reputation as the

"Apostle of Pan-Destruction." The appellation was not entirely deserved. Although he might be justifiably dubbed the father of revolutionary anarchism, he still talked of a new and better humanity arising from the bloody ruins of destruction.

Far more characteristic of the ruthless dedication to violent behavior was Bakunin's follower, Sergei Nechayev. Even though it was Bakunin who apparently composed the notorious *Catechism of the Revolutionist* (1869), it was Nechayev, in his daily machinations, who gave content to its distorted code of ethics. A few of the more malevolent paragraphs of that document deserve quotation.

> The revolutionist . . . knows only one science, the science of destruction. . . . The object is but one—the quickest possible destruction of that ignoble [social] system.

> To him whatever aids the triumph of the revolution is ethical; all that which hinders it is unethical and minimal.

> Day and night he must have one thought, one aim—inexorable destruction.

> To consolidate this world into one invincible, all-destroying force is the sole object of our organization.[29]

This document was to become the manual for those fanatical elements who combined terrorism and banditry with political purpose. But even this blood-curdling rationalization for violence did not specify that violence *per se* is to be applauded. There was no mention that this crass pragmatism is good for the individual psyche or that violence can mold and uplift a nation or a people. Rather it was held merely that violence is good for the "cause," because without it the destruction of the old order would not be possible. The fact that the ultimate end to be achieved was vaguely conceived, or that discussion of it was avoided does not detract from its conception of violence as being fundamentally instrumental.

This characteristic instrumentality of violence is even more evident in the preachments of anarchists in other countries at other times. Basic to their argument is the conviction that all forms of government rest on violence, and therefore government is wrong and harmful, as well as unnecessary. In posing the question, "Is Anarchism Violence?" the American Alexander Berkman responded:

> No, my friend, it is capitalism and government which stand for disorder and violence. Anarchism is the very reverse of it; it means order without government and peace without violence.

The hypothetical dialogue continues:

> Yes, anarchists have thrown bombs and have sometimes resorted to violence.
>
> But do not let us be too hasty. If anarchists have sometimes employed violence, does it necessarily mean that anarchism means violence?
> When a citizen puts on a soldier's uniform, he may have to throw bombs and use violence. Will you say, then, that citizenship stands for bombs and violence? You will indignantly resent the imputation. It simply means, you will reply, that *under certain conditions* a man may have to resort to violence. That man may happen to be a democrat, a monarchist, a socialist, Bolshevik, or anarchist.
>
> Anarchists have no monopoly on violence.[30]

Among American anarchists there has been a drift away from symbolic individualized acts of violence, the "propaganda by deed" position. The earlier Bakunin-Nechayev practices never achieved a widespread following. Violent acts, when they did come, demonstrated the perceived pragmatic qualities of violence in revolutionary anarchism.

One characteristic expression of the intrinsic ideology of violence is the view that violence is noble, heroic, and hence moral. Violence, in this context, gives meaning to one's life. Violence and heroism have been integrally linked in many cultures, certainly in our own. A person can be a hero because of his behavior in a violent activity, especially warfare. A person can also be a hero because of his capacity for non-violence, especially in the face of violent provocation, although this facet of heroism is less widely recognized in our society. A person can be a hero by enduring or being struck down by someone else's violence in particular circumstances. This is especially the case if that person is already a public figure, as were John F. Kennedy and Malcolm X. By and large, however, heroic status is reserved for the one proficient in the use of violent techniques.

Such "masculine fantasies," as one commentator has called this adoration of violence, have run throughout modern Western thought and behavior. We find them everywhere: in the realities of male chauvinism, in the writings and posturing of a Norman Mailer and an Ernest Hemingway, in the *machismo* attributed to Latin American leaders, in the *Verbindungen* (fighting corps) of the German universities, in Nietzsche's *Zarathustra*, in the codes of chivalry, and in any number of contemporary manifestations. Referring to the recent wars that societies have fought, for example, one military analyst argues:"To eliminate conflict because it is risky is to eliminate all that is heroic in human existence. Life without this kind of conflict would be reduction of man's existence to the pre-human level, to life without quality."[33]

The glorification of violence assumed its most horrifying proportions in the fascist world, where not only was man regarded as being tested and made complete in battle, but a people, as a group, were thought to be tempered by violent challenge. Perhaps the definitive doctrinal expression of this philosophy was supplied by Benito Mussolini. "War alone," he wrote in his famous essay on the political and social doctrine of fascism, "brings up to its highest tension all human energy and puts the stamp of nobility upon the peoples who have the courage to meet it. All other trials are substitutes which never really put men into the postion where they have to make the great decision—the alternative of life or death."[34] Militaristic ideologies, especially Nazism, bring out this blood lust among men. One Reichswehr officer reflected metaphysically on his experiences in World War I:

> The war is the Father of all things, therefore, also our Father; war has forged us, marked us, formed us and hardened us, to make us what we are now. And always, as long as life's whirling wheel will rotate us, this war will be the very axis around which it will turn.[35]

This same officer went on to describe the struggle on the battlefield which "tore one irresistibly forward, and made the earnest and dark background of death appear more profound and intoxicating."[36] When this mentality drifted into the attribution of superior nation-building qualities to violent causes, it hit upon a responsive contemporary note. In Mao's doctrine of the protracted conflict we find a rationalization for violence, not simply because the time factor is regarded as a military ally that can assure the guerrilla forces ultimate victory, but because political strategy dictates that an effective state and governmental structure and a unified people will emerge from the crucible of extended struggle. This view was put succinctly by the late Eduardo Mondlane of Mozambique's FRELIMO, when he wrote:

> Paradoxically, the fact that the war will be drawn out in this way may in the long run be an advantage to our ultimate development. For war is an extreme of political action, which tends to bring about social change more rapidly than any other instrument; and in a country as backward as Mozambique, rapid social change will be essential after independence. [37]

"We do not like war," wrote another African nationalist revolutionary, "but this armed struggle has its advantages. Through it we are building a nation that is solid, conscious of itself."[38] But the fact remains that those who call for sacrifice and discipline from their followers, who invoke the noble analogy of a people united at war, are not singing the praises of violence *per se,* certainly not in the sense of the advocates of violence as an intrinsic good. Rather, since it is widely felt that a willingness to assume the risks of warfare is the highest test of a person's dedication to a cause, they are trying to demonstrate the *utility* of violent techniques to achieve "higher" ends. Sacrifice and heroism may be perceived as the essence of being. But it does not follow that devotion to violence *qua* violence brings out the best in a man.

For all of these except the more fuzzy-minded anarchists, violence was no substitute for program or strategy. Only among the more fanatical supporters was violence an unmitigated blessing. For an examination of the practical application of an intrinsic ideology of violence, we shall have to turn to the very antithesis of violence for violence's sake, to the pacifists who maintain and operate on the principle that violence is inherently evil, destructive of the humanity of man.

Pacifism

Just as there is a qualitative difference between the employment of violent techniques and the glorification of violence *per se*, so there is an important qualitative difference between those who use non-violent methods because they think that tactically non-violence will"work," and those who are committed to pacifism as an absolute and principled denial of violence in any form. Obviously dedicated pacifists do not divorce the question of violence as a good or evil from its social context. Rather pacifists are intrinsic ideologists in the sense that they do not discuss the issues on the pragmatic or expedient grounds of tactics and strategy, but at the abstract level of principle and morality. To be sure, there may be perfectly rational, practical reasons that lend credence to their case. But that is not their chief perceived motive.

On the other hand, the pacifism we wish to explore is not strictly an intellectualized pacifism, more comfortable with discussion that with political action. The pacifists we wish to treat have demonstrated their determination to actualize their ideals, to risk their bodies and treasures, to suffer ostracization and rejection. Take, for example, the teachings and actions of Mohandas K. Gandhi. His commitment to *Ahimsa*, or non-violence, was completely bound up in his religious ideals. For this reason, non-violence is not simply the abhorrence of violence. If that were the case practically all of us would be pacifists. However, the doctrine of *Ahimsa* contains a second, a positive facet. To Gandhi, *Ahimsa* was the heart of all religion. He held that the truth of all life on earth and of God himself is to be found in the principle of the sacredness of all life and the refusal to use violence. But *Ahimsa* is not simply a negative virtue, that is, a denial of action of a refusal to do harm. Rather, it involves an equally compelling commitment to do good to living things. *Ahimsa*, in other words, is supreme kindness and supreme self-sacrifice. This Soul-Force, or *Satyagraha*, makes ostensibly a negative act into a positive human force. To fully understand the religious basis of Gandhi's thought and the second, often neglected, propelling facet, it is helpful to quote the Mahatma at length.

> All life in the flesh exists by some violence. Hence the highest religion has been defined by a negative word, Ahimsa. The world is bound in a chain of destruction. In other words, violence is an inherent necessity for life in the body. That is why a votary of Ahimsa always prays for ultimate deliverance from the bondage of the flesh.
>
> But every seeker after truth has to adjust and vary the standard according to the individual need, and to make a ceaseless endeavor to reduce the circle of violence.
>
> Non-violence works in a most mysterious manner. Often a man's actions defy analysis in terms of non-violence; equally often his actions may wear the appearance of violence when he is absolutely non-violent in the highest sense of the term, and is subsequently found to be so.
>
> For me non-violence is not a mere philosophical principle. It is the rule and the breath of my life. I know I fail often, sometimes consciously, more often unconsciously. It is a matter not of the intellect but of the heart. True guidance comes by constant waiting upon God, by utmost humility, self-abnegation, by being ever ready to sacrifice one's self. Its practice requires fearlessness and courage of the highest order.
>
> But the light within me is steady and clear. There is no escape for any of us save through truth and non-violence. I know that war is wrong, is an unmitigated evil. I know, too, that it has got to go. I firmly believe that freedom won through bloodshed or fraud is no freedom.[39]

There is something of a danger in quoting Gandhi. He was not always consistent in his teachings.[40] Even in these passages one can grasp the torture of his mind as he grappled with the dilemma of life being in the flesh and *Ahimsa* being a principle rooted in the spirit. He tried to reconcile this strictly in religious and philosophical terms. But in practice he realized that reconciliation might well be a process of trial and error, of human failing as well as achievement. Gandhi was never a literalist. He often said that life involved sometimes the choice between the lesser of evils. He was generally indifferent to charges of inconsistency, for he knew that Soul-Force must prevail. In him it did.

The religious Society of Friends (Quakers) have for years adhered to a similar code of behavior. It is exemplified not simply by their repeated refusals to bear arms or fight, but by their diverse community "concerns." It is propelled, as was Gandhi, by a belief that there exists "that of God in every-man," or an "Inner Light" as it is sometimes called within each person, and that "Light" must be made to shine outward toward others with whom that person comes into contact. Thus in the final message of the All Friends Conference in London, 1920, Gandhi's universal views take solid root in unorthodox Christian soil.

> The Christianity which makes war impossible is a way of life which extirpates or controls the dispositions that lead to war. It eradicates the seeds of war in one's daily life. . . . It is not consistent for anyone to claim that his way of life stops him from war unless he is prepared to adjust his entire life in its personal aspirations, in its relationships with his fellows, in its pursuits of truth, in its economic and social bearings, in its political obligation, in its religious fellowships, in its intercourse with God—to the tremendous demands of Christ's way.[41]

Such pacificism is rooted in the acceptance of the doctrine of unconditional love for all men. One can never wholly reject any man, no matter how despicable his actions may be, since love of one's fellow man is not conditioned by the fulfillment of certain demands, such as obedience, confession of sin, membership in a particular church, or professed belief in some real or symbolic deity. There are no heretics, pagans, or sinners who must be rejected, saved, or punished. If one first accepts the concept of "God in every man," then it follows that the negation of humanism, that is physical or psychological violation, are to be rejected in toto, and what is more, positive humanitarian acts must be performed (and not in the patronizing sense).

Among the many people today who purport to be non-violent there are some who tend to lack the second ingredient of a viable pacificism, a spiritual "Soul-Force," and obvious "Inner Light," that is necessary to carry them through to victory. In contrast, time and again, faced by malicious provocation, Gandhi relied upon his inner strength to obtain his object. He refused to turn to physical force. The acts of a lifetime, one great passive resistance movement after another, where he eschewed violent options, even the options of compulsion, to attain his ends, are testimony enough to his spiritual power.

Passive resistance was forged into a powerful social and political tool in India. Gandhi's followers did not always understand his teachings and many who did understand him were not strong enough spiritually to resist the realities of the flesh. Gandhi was aware of this danger. In response to the view that practically speaking passive resistance was a weapon of the weak, Gandhi was grudgingly obliged to agree. "With me alone and a few other co-workers it came out of our strength and was described as satyagraha, but with the majority it was purely and simply passive resistance . . . because they were too weak to undertake methods of violence."[42] But beneath the weakness there lies the underlying threat of massive violence, the possibility that followers without inner strength might "break," that passive resistance might get out of hand. This is a possibility whenever it is employed. For the British, and for Gandhi and his closest associates it was a source of constant worriment. The impact of the possibility of massive violence on Gandhi's opponents cannot be discounted. But nevertheless, it remains that this postmodern ideology of violence, which embodies the negation of violence, became this form of ideology's most powerful, and in practical terms its most successful, expression.

NOTES

1. Norman Mailer, "Talking of Violence," *20th Century* (Winter 1964-65): 110.

2. Ibid., p. 109.

3. Ibid., p. 111.

4. Ibid.

5. Colin Wilson, "Crimes of Freedom—and Their Cure," *20th Century* (Winter 1964-65): 29.

6. Ibid., p. 28.

7. Jack Lively, *The Works of Joseph de Maistre* (New York: The Macmillan Company, 1965), p. 62.

8. Ibid., p. 63.

9. Georges Sorel, *Reflections on Violence* (New York: Peter Smith, 1941), p. 195.

10. Ibid., p.200.

11. Ibid., p. 298.

12. Ibid., p. 46.

13. Ibid., p. 121.

14. Ibid., p. 90.

15. Ibid., p. 99.

16. Ibid., p. 298.

17. Ibid., pp. 98-99.

18. Frantz Fanon, *The Wretched of the Earth* (New York: Grove Press, 1968), p. 36.

19. Ibid., p. 38.

20. Ibid., p. 41.

21. Ibid., p. 53.

22. Ibid., p. 37.

23. Ibid., p. 92.

24. Ibid., p. 93.

25. Ibid., p. 86.

26. Ibid., pp. 36-37.

27. Ibid., p. 94.

28. Quoted from "Reaction in Germany," *Deutsche Jahrbücher* (1842) in Max Nomad (Podolsky), *Apostles of Revolution* (Boston: Little, Brown & Co., 1939), p. 149.

29. Ibid., pp. 228,228,229, and 233. The entire document is reprinted therein, pp. 228-33.

30. All quotations are from Berkman's *ABC of Anarchism* (1929), excerpts of which are reprinted in: Henry J. Silverman, ed., *American Radical Thought* (Lexington, Mass.: D.C. Heath, 1970), pp. 178-95.

31. Ali A. Mazrui, *Violence and Thought: Essays on Social Tensions in Africa* (New York: Humanities Press, 1969), p. 200.

32. William V. Shannon, "Notes on Violence," *New York Times*, 21 October 1971, p. 47.

33. Anthony Harrigan, *Defence Against Total Attack* (Cape Town: Nasionale Boekhandel Bpk., 1965), p. 12.

34. "Fascismo," in *Enciclopedia Italiana*, Vol. XIV (1932 edition).

35. Ernst Jünger as quoted in Harrigan, *Defence Against Total Attack*, p. 32. Although Jünger extolled heroism in war in his diary, *Storm of Steel* (1929), he soon became a critic of the Third Reich in *On the Marble Cliffs* (1950), originally published in German in 1939.

36. Ibid., p. 33. A more visceral expression of this attitude can be found in the writing of Mussolini's son, Vittorio, growing out of his air force experiences in Ethiopia. See: G.A. Borgese, *Goliath: The March of Fascism* (New York: Viking, 1938), pp. 432-33.

37. Eduardo Mondlane, *The Struggle for Mozambique* (Harmondsworth: Penguin, 1969), p. 219.

38. Amilcar Cabral, "Foreword" to Basil Davidson, *The Liberation of Guinea: Aspects of an African Revolution* (Harmondsworth: Penguin, 1969), p. 13.

39. From C.F. Andrews, *Mahatma Gandhi's Ideas, Including Selections from His Writings* (New York: Macmillan, 1930), pp. 138, and 142-43.

40. For example, the African National Congress, a South African revolutionary nationalist party, takes pride in numbering Gandhi among its founders by quoting the following 1938 statement by him: "Where the choice is set between cowardice and violence I would advise violence. . . . This is because he who runs away commits mental violence; he has not the courage of facing death by killing. I would a thousand times prefer violence than the emasculation of a whole race. I prefer to use arms in defense of honour than remain the vile witness of dishonour." See: "From Gandhi to Mandela," *Sechaba* (London), III, No, 5 (May, 1969), p. 10.

41. Philadelphia Yearly Meeting of the Religious Society of Friends, *Faith and Practice* (Philadelphia: Author, 1961), pp. 224-25. A provocative treatment of these themes can be found in: Elbert W. Russell, "Christianity and Militarism," *Peace Research Reviews* 4 (November 1971): 1-80. See also, Elbert Russell, *The History of Quakerism* (New York: Macmillan, 1942); Roland H. Bainton, *Christian Attitudes Toward War and Peace* (New York: Abingdon, 1960); and Howard H. Brinton, *Friends for 300 Years* (Philadelphia: Pendle Hill Publications, 1964).

42. As quoted in Erik H. Erikson, *Gandhi's Truth: On the Origins of Militant Nonviolence* (New York: W.W. Norton, 1969), p. 372.

Chapter Six

Perspectives and Findings

The preceding analysis of the ideologies of violence used a distinctive method which does not neatly fit into any of the categories under which political scientists normally classify work done in their discipline. The situational method employed throughout the discussion aimed at providing a description of how the different justifications of violence are manipulated in concrete political situations. Thus, its goal was neither a causal analysis describing the conditions under which particular justifications of political violence arise, nor ethical appraisal of the various justifications of violence. It is much more a guide to the ways in which political actors rationalize and condemn violence in attempts to win support for their policies. Its ultimate use is perhaps as an antidote to quick belief in any justification or condemnation of violence. Thus, the situational method is both critical and empirical.

Criticism

At the root of the situational method is criticism of political rhetoric. However, this criticism departs from the two most prevalent ways of analyzing political rhetoric. Normally, ideologies are criticized either from the viewpoint of sociology of knowledge or that of philosophical anthropology. The sociology of knowledge approach traces ideologies to such "causal" variables as economic class interest or position within power structures. Under this interpretation, political rhetoric is "conditioned" by underlying interests and is merely a "reflection" and expression of those interests. The philosophical anthropology approach moves in an opposite direction and criticizes political rhetoric in terms of moral standards deemed valid. The aim of philosophical anthropology is knowledge of "the good life," and ideologies are the raw materials out of which this knowledge may be culled.

As we engage in it, situational analysis is neither sociology of knowledge nor philosophical anthropology. In numerous instances throughout the discussion it has been shown that the same or closely similar ideologies of violence have been used by the most implacable political foes. For example, self-avowed revolutionary Marxists have used legitimist ideologies to justify their uses of force in certain situations (particularly when they are in control of the state), just as the dominant white South African elite has sometimes resorted to pluralist justifications. "Revolutionary" elites in the emerging nations have sometimes used the very same expansionist justifications of violence as the hated colonial oppressors. These instances would seem to challenge the sociology of knowledge claim that any particular kinds of interests solely determine the content of ideologies, though they certainly do not challenge the broader realist claim that ideologies are often weapons in political conflict. Situational analysis also does not pass judgment on the justifications of violence in terms of some "higher" standard. There is no intended presumption guiding this study that violence is evil and non-violence good, or the reverse. Also, there is no intention to judge whether or not specific political actors are offering justifications of violence in good faith.

Moreover, it must be constantly borne in mind that this sort of analysis does not absolve the observer or the moral critic from the responsibility of examining the normative content of each ideological contestant. We are concentrating on violence in various ideological modes and not on the normative issues here. Otherwise, it would be preposterous to group together, for example, the white supremacists of South Africa and the anti-racists from various liberation movements. There are indeed similarities in the rhetorical styles and in their applications of ideology, but there are also profound differences, differences that put them miles apart in the social orders they strive to maintain or to achieve.

How, then, is situational analysis critical? The basis of criticism in situational analysis is that ideologies tend to "mystify" by claiming that certain situations make the use of violence or the abstention from violence absolutely necessary. There are many ways of interpreting this necessity, each of which is subject to criticism. One familiar use of "is" and "must" by ideologists of violence is that some acts of violence are "inevitable." For example, legitimists often maintain that violence necessarily breeds counter-violence. This appears to be on the surface a social scientific law of questionable validity. However, the purpose of the ideologist is scarcely to offer an hypothesis to be empirically verified. Rather, the aim is to persuade dissidents not to use violence and, perhaps, to justify counter-violence by defenders of the establishment. A similar process, though in reverse, works for revolutionaries who state the "fact" that violence is "pervasive" in a given society. They do not make this statement to promote knowledge for its own sake, but to justify the use of violence by dissidents and to condemn the "hypocritical" defenders of the establishment. Behind these two arguments, and all similar ones, are hidden moral assumptions, including the assumption that the "eye for an eye" morality is valid, and the view that violence in the propagation of a "just" cause is justifiable.

A second use of "is" and "must" is the claim that certain acts of violence are morally necessary, or even obligatory. Examples of this kind of argument abound in the ideologies of violence. Revolutionaries like Merleau-Ponty try to make certain acts of violence morally obligatory by arguing that one has the choice of either participating in the violence of the oppressed or implicating oneself in the pervasive violence of the oppressor. In any case, participation in violence in inescapable. One is faced merely with a choice as to which form of violence he will sanction. Even so, since oppression is presumably immoral, the only moral alternative is to cast one's lot with the oppressed, who are engaged in violence with the intent of putting an end to violence. Similarly, moral necessity is used by apologists for cultural expansion. Such ideologists argue that one has the choice of using violence as a tool of defending and expanding a superior civilization, or of refraining from violence and witnessing the conquest of civilization by barbarians. Just as questionable moral assumptions were behind statements about the inevitability of violence, questionable factual assumptions are behind statements about the moral necessity of violence. Revolutionaries often suppose that societies are neatly divided into oppressors and oppressed, and that violence is an effective tool through which liberation of the oppressed can be achieved. Similarly, chauvinists suppose that societies are neatly divided into civilized and barbarous, and that violence is an effective tool for defending and expanding civilization. Further, all arguments for the moral necessity of violence assume that the end justifies the means.

A third use of "is" and "must" is that certain uses of violence have necessary effects on human beings. For example, some legitimists argue that when someone resorts to violence in order to redress a grievance, he inevitably becomes just like his enemy. Ironically, this argument is shared by pacifists, too. But whereas the legitimist advances this point for instrumental purposes, the pacifist regards it as intrinsically sound. Diametrically opposed to this interpretation are certain other ideologists who see violence as an in-trinsic part of a life-style and who claim that when oppressed people resort to violence against their oppressors they inevitably gain in dignity and other positive features of mental health. According to this view, oppressors, of course, merely become even more depraved by resorting to violence against the oppressed. The very existence of these contradictory claims casts doubt on both of them. It is probably correct that sometimes violence results in depr-avity and sometimes it results in liberation and dignity. However, the condi-tions in which these different results occur are not known and ideologists sel-dom deal in probabilities.

The situational method is critical because it attacks the claims of inevita-bility and necessity made by ideologists of violence. It attacks these claims primarily be placing them alongside one another, revealing their tacit as-sumptions and showing how they are used in political conflict. Thus, the sit-uational method demystifies absolutes and frees people to make more in-telligent responses and commitments to political activity. However, while it seeks to immunize people to propaganda, it also probably has the effect of making action more tentative and commitment to clear-cut positions more difficult. A tendency towards skepticism is the bias of this method, and it is important to realize that this bias is likely to make the method unacceptable to people who demand certainty in political action. It is also not calculated to appeal to those who find the "will to believe" a useful tactic for mobilizing bodies. In sum, the situational method is empirical, and ideologies are usu-ally anti-empirical; the situational method is skeptical, and certainty is one of the ideologist's motivating currencies.

Empiricism

In the process of criticizing pretensions to certainty, the situational method reveals how ideologies of violence are used as weapons in concrete political conflicts. There is a working assumption that political actors tend to use ideologies that are instrumental in accomplishing their general aims. This assumption helps make sense of the ways in which definitions of violence and justifications of violence are manipulated by political actors.

A hallmark of the situational method is its refusal to adopt any definition of political violence as either scientifically or morally superior to any other. This refusal is necessary so that definitions of violence themselves can be made variables in the analysis of political situations. Thus, rather than re-sulting in a judgment about which definition of violence is the best or most useful one, the situational method describes how the various definitions of violence relate to one another and how they are manipulated by political actors.

In general, definitions of violence can be classified on a continuum from restrictive to broad. The most restrictive definitions tend to confine violence to those uses of physical force which are prohibited by a normative order presumed to be legitimate, while the broadest definitions expand violence to all deprivations of asserted human rights. In between these poles is the definition of violence as any use of physical force. Ideologists tend to manipulate these definitions in accordance with their broader political aims. The most basic pattern is for defenders of constituted authority to use more restrictive definitions of violence and for opponents to constituted authority to use broader definitions of violence. The reason for this is fairly obvious. Those who oppose established authority frequently lack economic resources and control of communications networks. When they use physical force to further their aims they would like to put it in a context in which it appears as a reaction to oppression. This can be done by calling economic inequalities and even the established socialization process "violence." Thus, physical force loses any special status as an evil that it might have had, and becomes a justifiable reaction to other forms of violence. On the other hand, defenders of constituted authority usually do have economic resources and control of communications networks. They would like illegal uses of physical force to have a special status as an evil and "legitimate" force to be raised to the level of commendable action. Therefore, they tend to exclude everything but physical force used against the established order from the definition of violence. In between these two positions are liberal democrats who define violence as any use of physical force, because they would like to justify revolutions against authoritarian regimes which do not have built-in mechanisms for "peaceful change."

Manipulation of these definitions occurs when an ideologist or movement goes from one to another over time, or when two definitions are used by an ideologist simultaneously. An example of the first kind of manipulation is the shift from broad to restrictive definitions of violence by former opposition movements after they gain power. Once a revolutionary movement has become the constituted authority it finds it difficult, if not impossible, to argue that the use of physical force by dissidents is merely a response to economic and psychological violence of the regime. The use of two definitions simultaneously by an ideologist is also widespread. For example, revolutionaries frequently use a broad definition of violence when they are justifying their own uses of physical force and a more selective definition when they are criticizing force employed by agents of the establishment or when they are scampering for legal shelter from excessive regime violence, for example, police brutality or illegal searches or seizures. Thus, riots are sometimes justified as responses to structural violence, while police response to them is condemned as excessive and illegal violence. Similarly, defenders of constituted authority use a restricted definition of violence when justifying the use of force against dissenters and, frequently, a broader definition of violence when condemning dissenters; never so broad, however, as to include regime violence or structural violence. Thus, action against the opposition is legitimate force, while non-forceful demonstrations by the opposition are violent in the sense that they block streets or impede access to buildings.

In addition to using definitions of violence as weapons in political conflict, ideologists manipulate the various justifications of violence to rationalize the ways in which their allies use power. Here the basic pattern is far more apparent, because it is the very ground of this book. Ideologists supporting constituted authorities will tend to push towards legitimist justifications of violence, while ideologists supporting dissidents will tend to press towards pluralist justifications. Expansionist and intrinsic justifications are more unstable and tend to be related to the other two. The appeal of legitimist and pluralist justifications to ideologists is that they allow for rationalization in terms of a universal morality. For example, if the ideologist can get people to believe that there is only one "natural" or "legitimate" normative order, and that his allies represent it, much more than half of his battle is won. Given this context, people will view departures from the normative order by opposition groups not as promising alternatives and initiatives or tolerable experiments, but as condemnable deviations from the good social order. Adherence to the distinction between the legitimate force of the state and the illegitimate violence of the dissenters (enemies) will follow close on the heels of this attitude. Pluralist justifications universalize in a different way. Rather than claiming the universality of a particular normative order, they claim the universality of the right of each group to determine freely its own normative order. Here the context is diametrically opposed to the one prepared by the legitimist. No longer are departures from established ways viewed as condemnable deviations from the good life. Instead they are justifiable initiatives which represent the drive towards self-determination. The idea that violence is justified against oppressors who stand in the way of self-determination is closely related to this attitude.

Expansionist and intrinsic justifications appear when the other two begin to break down. Expansionist justifications are used by legitimist ideologists when it is no longer possible to pretend that the established order is natural or universal. It then becomes necessary to argue that it is superior in some way to competing orders. This justification begins to break down when superior force becomes the measure of moral superiority. Intrinsic justifications are used by pluralist ideologists who are interested in bringing new recruits into their movements, strengthening the resolve of current members, and terrorizing the opposition. Intrinsic justifications are ways of making people see the benefits that violence (or non-violence) can bring their personalities.

Once the people have been brought into the movement pluralist justifications are likely to take over.

There is perhaps an overall tendency which relates ideologies of violence to the power of groups. The less effective the opposition to a group is, the more the dominant group is likely to use legitimist justifications and narrow definitions of violence. Thus, legitimist justifications and narrow definitions are associated with effective, meaning stable and widely popular, ruling classes. As a group meets opposition, it becomes more likely to resort to expansionist justifications and broader definitions. If the group is fighting an up-hill battle, pluralist justifications and yet wider definitions are likely, and if the group is poorly organized and weak, intrinsic justifications and the widest definitions of violence become more likely. These are merely tendency statements, but they help account for many of the shifts and twists in ideologies that have been described in the preceding discussion.

The Problem in Justifying Violence

There is one further fundamental problem encountered by the ideologist who attempts to justify violence. However he defines the term violence, the ideologist must distinguish between the violent acts of friends and the violent acts of enemies. Thus, his aim is not to determine in the abstract which acts of violence are morally praiseworthy and which ones are blameworthy, but to justify acts of violence committed by his friends and condemn acts of violence committed by his enemies. Further, if he is to be effective, he must accomplish this aim while appearing to use universal moral standards. The one thing that he cannot do is state that the violence of friend and foe differ only in the fact that they are committed by different people or groups. There must be something special about the friend that distinguishes his violence from that of the foe.

The crudest way of dealing with this problem is simply to assume that friend is morally superior to foe. For example, the ideologist may assume that his audience will agree that an act of violence was justified simply because it was committed in the name of the proletariat, by a German against a Jew, or in defense of the Constitution. When such an assumption cannot be made, the ideologist can move in either of two directions. He can attempt to demonstrate in some way that friend is in fact morally superior to foe, and that this superiority justifies the use of violence by friends. It has not been a major concern of this book to show how ideologists attempt to demonstrate moral superiority for their side. A full discussion of this question would demand a critique of ideology in general, rather than merely a discussion of the ideologies of violence. The second direction in which the ideologist can move is to argue that there is something inherently superior about the violence used by his friends when it is compared to the violence of enemies. This kind of argument is at the core of ideologies of violence and has been referred to in many contexts throughout the preceding discussion.

In each of the major types of ideologies of violence, justifications appear which claim that there is something about certain acts of violence which makes them inherently praiseworthy. This kind of justification occurs in legitimist and pluralist ideologies which assume that violence is normally blameworthy, as well as in expansionist and intrinsic ideologies which sometimes seem to assume that violence is normally praiseworthy. In each case, the argument that there is inherent value to some acts of violence is the last resort of the ideologist. It also tends to take him beyond ideology.

For legitimist spokesmen the last resort is to argue that the violence of authorities is justified because it neutralizes the violence of private citizens and groups. Thus, violence is justified when it tends to limit the quantity of violent acts. This argument tends to take one beyond ideology because it is really not a case for the violence of a particular group, but a case for the necessity of government in general. It is ultimately an argument that can be used effectively only against anarchists. Any other opposition group could claim that if it took over the state it would neutralize violence even more effectively than the present authorities. Further, it is a standard which puts established authorities on continuous trial. If they fail to neutralize violence they have no right to rule. Putting one's friends on a performance test is something that ideologists attempt to avoid like the plague. This is perhaps why Hobbes, who is the greatest exponent of the neutralization argument, never won favor as an ideologist. Whatever his actual intention too many people read him to mean that sometimes it is expedient to obey the authorities because a minimum of public order is a necessary condition for fulfilling any other plans.

The final resort of the pluralist ideologist is quite similar to that of the legitimist. Instead of arguing that his allies are minimizing violence in the present, he maintains that his friends will minimize violence in the future, or eliminate it from public affairs altogether. He pictures the choice as being between the forces dedicated to perpetuating violence indefinitely and those intending to bring a halt to it. Unlike the neutralization argument, this one remains ideological because it is ultimately based on faith that the noble experiment of abolishing violence will work.

For expansionists the last resort is to make successful violence itself the mark of a superior normative order. This argument clearly takes one beyond ideology, because according to its standard one must deem superior whoever is successful. This is not troublesome so long as one's allies are successful, but it becomes embarrassing when they are in danger of defeat. The notion that success is its own excuse for being is a pitfall for almost any ideology of violence based on the denial that violence is normally blameworthy. This is why expansionist ideologies tend to be related to the breakdown of legitimist justifications. It is nearly the same thing to say that violence of the state is justified because it neutralizes other violence and that success in using violence is the mark of superiority. The expansionist is merely more clear-headed about the possibility that a number of groups might succeed in neutralizing the violence of the others.

The intrinsic justification for violence is always at the last resort because it argues that violence is a desirable component of a life-style rather than arguing that it is a mere means to a desirable end—the initial strategy of the other justifications. In a sense, it must work its way into ideology rather than beyond it, because its problem is to show that it is healthy for some people to use violence and detrimental for others. This is a difficult trick to turn because the intrinsic justification is the only one that individuals can test for themselves at any time. Anyone can find out for himself whether violence liberates or enslaves, whether non-violence strengthens personality or weakens it. This is why intrinsic ideologies are closely related to and dependent upon pluralist justifications. Intrinsic justifications are invitations to engage in collective action which has ulterior aims to the goal of self-development through violence or non-violence.

The last resort of ideologists of violence is to make claims about the effects of violence upon violence. It is here that the elasticity of their arguments becomes the greatest and their mystifications the most striking. The legitimist argues that the violence of the state neutralizes the violence of others, but conveniently forgets that the violence of others may be motivated by hatred of the state. The expansionist argues that right never triumphs unless served by might, and then turns around and makes might the only index of right. The pluralist stands against oppression and for self-determination and then sanctifies the violence of certain groups because it is supposedly aimed at ending violence altogether. The intrinsic ideologist claims that he knows in advance which people violence will liberate and which ones it will enslave, or that nobody will be liberated by violence. All of these paradoxes and tensions appear in contemporary political rhetoric. With the emergence of intrinsic ideologies, violence has exerted a profound hold on the twentieth century mind. Cults of violence have appeared side by side with militant non-violent movements. The situational method will not tell which one, if any, definition or justification of violence is the right one, but it may loosen the hold of violence on the mind through its critique of ideological pretensions. Somehow the issue of violence becomes less intoxicating. It is no longer dogmatized or absolutized.